Every Day Counts®

Daily Planning Guide: Fostering Effective Discussion

Includes:

- Daily Discussion Questions
- Weekly Planning Charts for Calendar Math
- Intervention
- Helpful Hints
- Benchmark and Monthly Assessments

Grade 3

MW01235948

GR
SO
HOUGHTO

Copyright © 2012 by Houghton Mifflin Harcourt Publishing Company

All rights reserved. No part of this work may be reproduced or transmitted in any form or by any means, electronic or mechanical, including photocopying or recording, or by any information storage or retrieval system, without the prior written permission of the copyright owner unless such copying is expressly permitted by federal copyright law.

Permission is hereby granted to teachers using EVERY DAY COUNTS to photocopy tests and record forms from this publication in classroom quantities for instructional use and not for resale. Requests for information on other matters regarding duplication of this work should be addressed to Houghton Mifflin Harcourt Publishing Company, Attn: Contracts, Copyrights, and Licensing, 9400 South Park Center Loop, Orlando, Florida 32819.

Printed in the U.S.A.

ISBN 978-0-547-56983-3

4 5 6 7 8 9 10 0877 20 19 18 17 16 15 14 13 12

4500344970 A B C D E F G

If you have received these materials as examination copies free of charge, Houghton Mifflin Harcourt Publishing Company retains title to the materials and they may not be resold. Resale of examination copies is strictly prohibited.

Possession of this publication in print format does not entitle users to convert this publication, or any portion of it, into electronic format.

Table of Contents

© Houghton Mifflin Harcourt Publishing Company

How to Use This Planning Guide: Making the Most of Every Day Counts

What is this publication?

The *Every Day Counts® Daily Planning Guide* is designed to help teachers implement *Every Day Counts: Calendar Math* with fidelity and ease by providing discussion questions for each day, as well as Intervention, More Helpful Hints, and Assessment.

This planning guide helps teachers:

- distinguish between Update Questions and Discussion Questions.
- make the most of the 10–15 minutes of daily discussion.
- focus their discussion on key math topics daily.

All are included in this planning guide to make daily implementation of *Every Day Counts* more effective than ever.

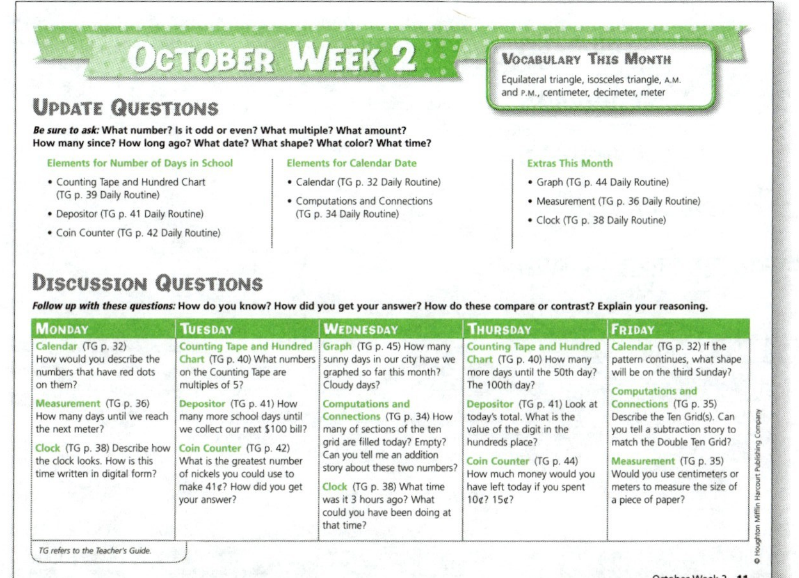

October Week 2

Vocabulary This Month
Equilateral triangle, isosceles triangle, A.M. and P.M., centimeter, decimeter, meter

Update Questions

Be sure to ask: **What number? Is it odd or even? What multiple? What amount? How many since? How long ago? What date? What shape? What color? What time?**

Elements for Number of Days in School
- Counting Tape and Hundred Chart (TG p. 39 Daily Routine)
- Depositor (TG p. 41 Daily Routine)
- Coin Counter (TG p. 42 Daily Routine)

Elements for Calendar Date
- Calendar (TG p. 32 Daily Routine)
- Computations and Connections (TG p. 34 Daily Routine)

Extras This Month
- Graph (TG p. 44 Daily Routine)
- Measurement (TG p. 36 Daily Routine)
- Clock (TG p. 38 Daily Routine)

Discussion Questions

Follow up with these questions: **How do you know? How did you get your answer? How do these compare or contrast? Explain your reasoning.**

Monday	Tuesday	Wednesday	Thursday	Friday
Calendar (TG p. 32) How would you describe the numbers that have red dots on them?	Counting Tape and Hundred Chart (TG p. 40) What numbers on the Counting Tape are multiples of 5?	Graph (TG p. 45) How many sunny days in our city have we graphed so far this month? Cloudy days?	Counting Tape and Hundred Chart (TG p. 40) How many more days until the 50th day? The 100th day?	Calendar (TG p. 32) If the pattern continues, what shape will be on the third Sunday?
Measurement (TG p. 36) How many days until we reach the next meter?	Depositor (TG p. 41) How many more school days until we collect our next $100 bill?	Computations and Connections (TG p. 34) How many of sections of the ten grid are filled today? Empty? Can you tell me an addition story about these two numbers?	Depositor (TG p. 41) Look at today's total. What is the value of the digit in the hundreds place?	Computations and Connections (TG p. 35) Describe the Ten Grid(s). Can you tell a subtraction story to match the Double Ten Grid?
Clock (TG p. 38) Describe how the clock looks. How is this time written in digital form?	Coin Counter (TG p. 42) What is the greatest number of nickels you could use to make 41¢? How did you get your answer?	Clock (TG p. 38) What time was it 3 hours ago? What could you have been doing at that time?	Coin Counter (TG p. 44) How much money would you have left today if you spent 10¢? 15¢?	Measurement (TG p. 35) Would you use centimeters or meters to measure the size of a piece of paper?

TG refers to the Teacher's Guide.

© Houghton Mifflin Harcourt Publishing Company

What is the difference between Update Questions and Discussion Questions?

Update Questions are those asked quickly and daily to update the board, and usually require only one-word answers. They are recall questions and often do not require high-level thinking. Questions for updates are similar to, "What is the day's date? What day is it? What month is it? How many days have we been in school? What is the pattern piece on the Calendar? How much money do we have today? What is the amount in the Depositor today? How many feet do we have so far?"

> **Remember:** It is important to update every element daily, but it is not necessary to hold a discussion about every element every day.

Discussion Questions require higher level thinking such as comprehension, application, analysis, synthesis and evaluation. Examples of discussion questions are, "Can you explain your thinking? What information did you use to solve the problem? How would you compare and contrast? What would you predict? How can you prove it?"

© Houghton Mifflin Harcourt Publishing Company

How can I use the Daily Planning Guide?

Every Day Counts employs two numbers throughout the program: **Number of the Day in School** and **Date of the Month.**

The ***number of days in school*** refers to days students come to school, and in most schools this is about 180–200 days. This number grows continuously throughout the school year, starting with the first day of school (Day 1), and documenting each day that students are in attendance.

The ***date of the month*** follows the calendar. This number resets to one every month, so using the calendar date provides opportunities to work with small numbers over and over, whereas the number of the days in school is constantly growing.

How can I use these two numbers more effectively?

When holding *Every Day Counts* discussions, try not to jump back and forth from your *days in school* number to the *date of the month.* For example, when talking about today being the 14th day in school, discuss all elements that go with 14. When discussing the date of the month, discuss all the elements that focus on the date. This helps students make better connections to the numbers and all that they are asked to think about in relation to these numbers.

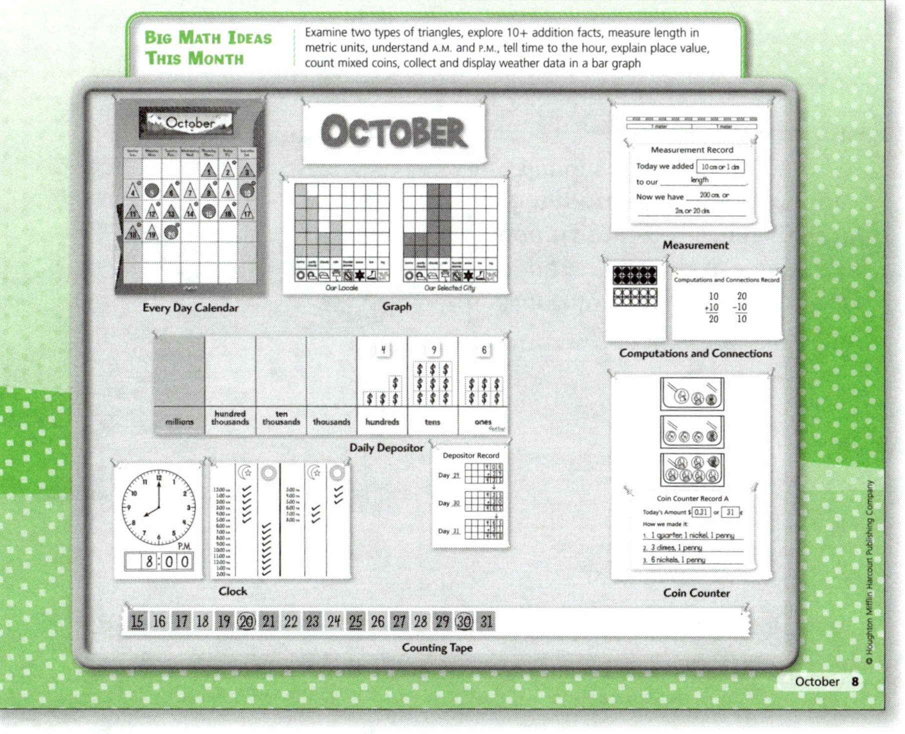

© Houghton Mifflin Harcourt Publishing Company

Monthly Overview

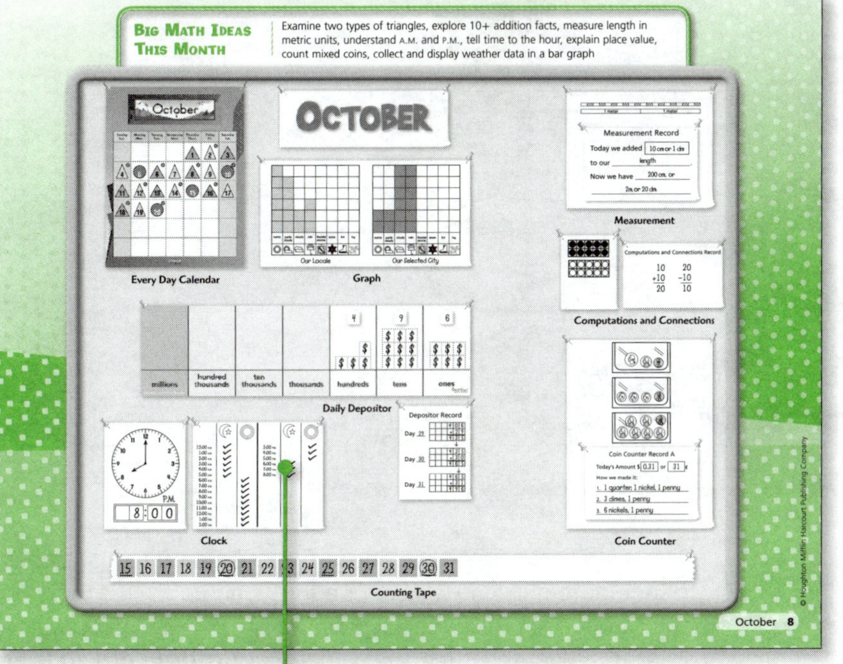

A "snapshot" of the coming month provides a quick visual reference of the elements that will be used in the month.

Monthly Resources offer more opportunities to use *Every Day Counts* in times other than the 15 minutes allotted daily for Calendar Math.

Helpful Hints encourage further use of *Every Day Counts* for practice and enrichment activities.

Intervention ideas use *Every Day Counts* to engage students deeper into the math while providing intervention on key concepts and skills.

Monthly Resources

Intervention

- **Multiples of 2, 5 and 10: Small Group:** This month, students will look at grouping the day's number on the Counting Tape by 2s, 5s, or 10s. While they may be able to count by 2s, 5s, or 10s, they may not realize that the day's number could be a multiple of one of these numbers. Review multiples as numbers that can be grouped by the given number or separated into groups of the given number. Use counters or the self-stick notes from the Counting Tape to check whether a given number is a multiple of 2, 5, or 10.
- **Difference Between Two Numbers: Small Group:** For students struggling with the mental math questions about the difference between the day's number and 100, begin with questions about the difference between the day's number and the next ten. Then ask questions about the difference between the day's number and the next 2 tens and so on. For example on Day 36, ask the difference between 36 and 40. Then ask the difference between 36 and 50. Ask the student to explain how he figured out the answer. Continue asking the difference between the day's number and the next greater ten until the number 100 has been reached. This same strategy can be helpful to obtain the total in the Depositor as well, since adding the day's amount is to be done mentally. Counting by 10s off the decade (e.g. 17, 27, 37, . . .) can also be helpful.

More Helpful Hints

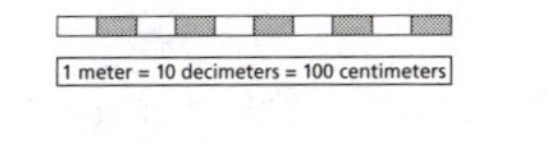

- Graph: At the end of the month, put the two graphs aside. You will need them in January, when graphs will be made for winter forecasts in the same two locations.
- Coin Counter: While *Calendar Math* provides play money cardstock and demonstration coins to place on the board, some teachers like to use real money or plastic money for the students to manipulate during discussions. Cutting egg cartons into thirds provides a container for each student. Each student will have storage for quarters, dimes, nickels and pennies; and four to eight containers stack nicely for storage.
- Measurement: Have students cut the 10 cm by 5 cm strips in advance and add one strip to the Measurement display in the classroom throughout the month. On days used to discuss Measurement, refer to the total that the students have mounted to match the day of the month.

1 meter = 10 decimeters = 100 centimeters

Assessments

October Assessment: See pages 77–80.
Addition Facts Progress Record: See page 111.
Assessment Checklist: See pages 109–110.

© Houghton Mifflin Harcourt Publishing Company

October 9

© Houghton Mifflin Harcourt Publishing Company

Weekly Planner

Update all elements daily with questions like these listed below.

The **date of the calendar** determines the number used for these elements.

Key vocabulary for each month is consolidated in one place.

The **number of days in school** determines the number used for these elements.

These are other elements to include in this month.

For more information on an element, refer to the indicated page in the *Every Day Counts* Teacher's Guide.

These questions are meant to take longer and encourage critical thinking and mathematical reasoning.

October Week 1

Vocabulary This Month

Equilateral triangle, isosceles triangle, A.M. and P.M., centimeter, decimeter, meter

Update Questions

Be sure to ask: **What number? Is it odd or even? What multiple? What amount? How many since? How long ago? What date? What shape? What color? What time?**

Elements for Number of Days in School

- Counting Tape and Hundred Chart (TG p. 39 Daily Routine)
- Depositor (TG p. 41 Daily Routine)
- Coin Counter (TG p. 42 Daily Routine)

Elements for Calendar Date

- Calendar (TG p. 32 Daily Routine)
- Computations and Connections (TG p. 34 Daily Routine)

Extras This Month

- Graph (TG p. 44 Daily Routine)
- Measurement (TG p. 36 Daily Routine)
- Clock (TG p. 38 Daily Routine)

Discussion Questions

Follow up with these questions: **How do you know? How did you get your answer? How do these compare or contrast? What is the relationship between *a* and *b*? Explain your reasoning.**

Monday	Tuesday	Wednesday	Thursday	Friday
Calendar (TG p. 32) How would you describe today's Calendar Piece? **Measurement** (TG p. 36) On what day will we reach one meter? How many centimeters are in one meter? **Clock** (TG p. 38) What time is shown on the clock? Is it A.M. or P.M.? Is it dark or light outside?	**Counting Tape and Hundred Chart** (TG p. 39) Is today's number odd or even? How many days has it been since the 12th day of school? **Depositor** (TG p. 41) How much will be added to the Depositor today? How did you find the total? Does anyone have a different way?	**Graph** (TG p. 44) How are we recording temperature this month? How will we determine how to color 82 degrees? 67 degrees? **Counting Tape and Hundred Chart** (TG p. 40) Explain why 6 has two Multiple Markers, one for 2 and one for 3. What are some other numbers that will have both a heart and a triangle? Why?	**Counting Tape and Hundred Chart** (TG p. 39) Tell a multiples of 2 story. Write the story, draw a picture and write the number sentence. **Clock** (TG p. 43) How can you estimate the time without seeing the clock up close?	**Calendar** (TG p. 32) Describe the difference triangles on the Calendar Pieces. **Coin Counter** (TG p. 42) How can you make 23¢ with 5 coins? **Computations and Connections** (TG p. 34) What number sentences describe today's Double Ten Grid?

TG refers to the Teacher's Guide.

© Houghton Mifflin Harcourt Publishing Company

October Week 1 10

© Houghton Mifflin Harcourt Publishing Company

Making Plans for Every Day Counts Calendar Math Discussion

Helpful Tips

- Questions are not posed about each element every day; rather, they are chosen carefully to go with each element.
- To use *Every Day Counts* with fidelity, it is helpful to create lesson plans. (See Teacher's Guide pages 10–11.) This planner provides you with the questions to aid in that effort.

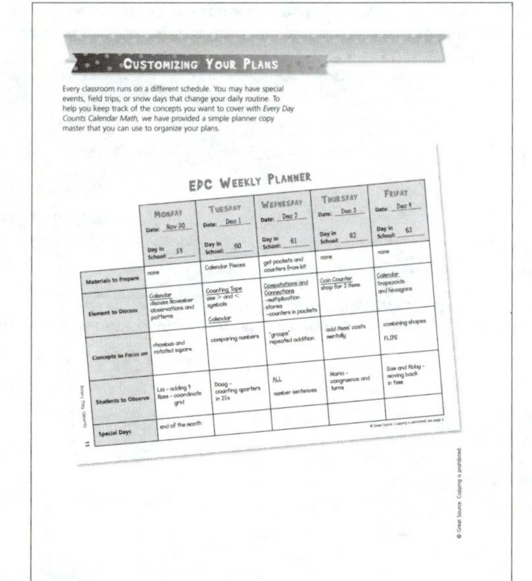

Customizing Your Plans

Every classroom runs on a different schedule. You may have special events, field trips, or snow days that change your daily routine. To help you keep track of the concepts you want to cover with *Every Day Counts Calendar Math,* we have provided a simple planner copy master that you can use to organize your plans.

EDC Weekly Planner

	Monday Date: Nov 30 Day in School: 59	Tuesday Date: Dec 1 Day in School: 60	Wednesday Date: Dec 2 Day in School: 61	Thursday Date: Dec 3 Day in School: 62	Friday Date: Dec 4 Day in School: 63
Materials to Prepare	none	Calendar Pieces	get pockets and counters from kit	none	none
Element to Discuss	Calendar discuss November observations and patterns	Counting Tape use > and < symbols Calendar	Computations and Connections -multiplication stories -counters in pockets	Coin Counter shop for 2 items	Calendar trapezoids and hexagons
Concepts to Focus on	rhombus and rotated square	comparing numbers	"groups" repeated addition	add items' costs mentally	combining shapes FLIPS
Students to Observe	Lia - adding 9 Ross - coordinate grid	Doug - counting quarters in 25s	ALL number sentences	Maria - congruence and turns	Sam and Abby - moving back in time
Special Days	end of the month				

10 Customizing Your Plans

11 Every Day Counts

- By planning your questions, the time spent on *Every Day Counts* will be more productive in furthering the mathematics being taught from the calendar.
- Upfront planning helps balance the time spent on each element.
- Update Questions are just used to cover the day's date and the day in school.
- Discussion Questions require higher cognitive skills and provide for more in-depth discussions.

Monthly Elements Discussion

The weekly charts follow a structure to ensure discussion of all the elements on a weekly basis.

- On **Mondays and Fridays,** questions are planned to go with ***date of the month,*** such as the Calendar, and other elements such as Daily Depositor (K), Coin Counter (1), Computations and Connections (2 and 3), Daily Depositor (4) and Fraction a Day (5).
- On **Tuesdays and Thursdays**, questions are planned to go with the ***number of days in school,*** such as the Counting Tape and other elements such as Clip Collection (K), Ten Grids (1), Coin Counter (2), Daily Depositor (3), Coin Counter (4), and Daily Decimal (5).
- On **Wednesdays,** questions are planned to go with Extra Elements, or to go more in depth with other elements such as Graphing.
- Some days will include discussions questions for elements outside the structure laid out above, for use in the classroom if time allows.

© Houghton Mifflin Harcourt Publishing Company

ASSESSMENT IN DAILY PLANNING GUIDE

Assessment items available as shown:

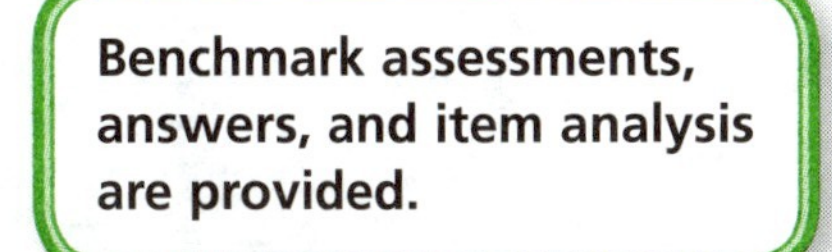

Benchmark assessments, answers, and item analysis are provided.

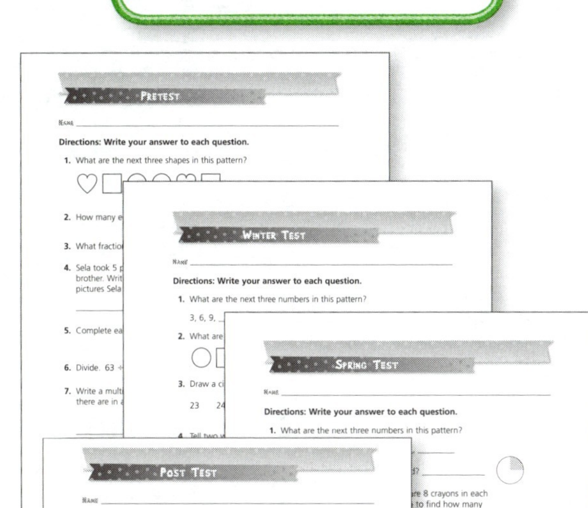

Use the Assessment Checklist to keep track of ongoing concept and skill mastery.

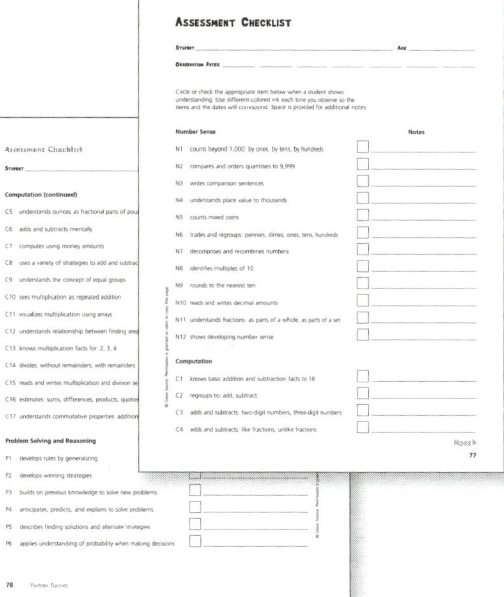

Students can be assessed on a monthly basis.

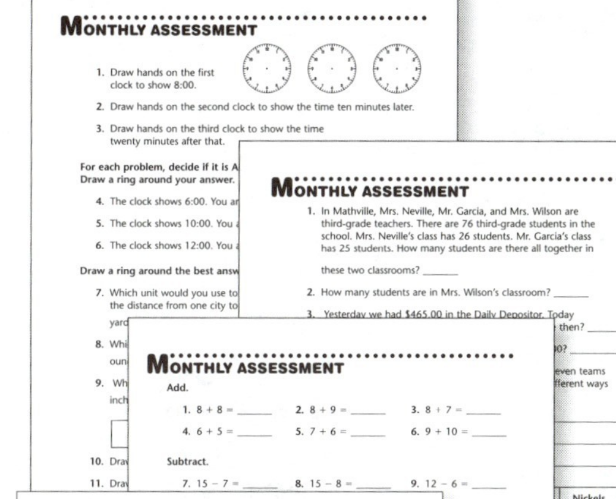

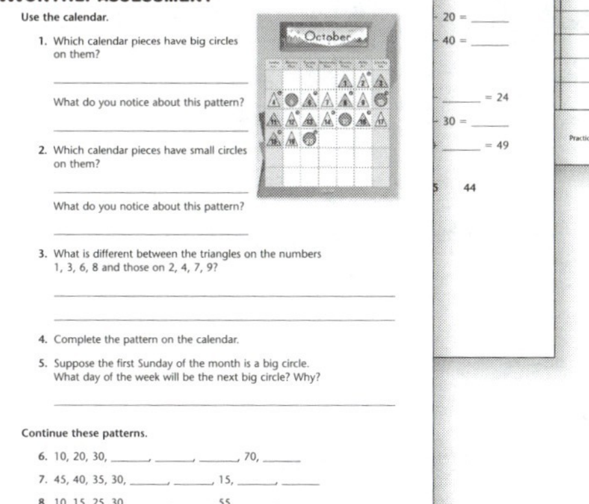

© Houghton Mifflin Harcourt Publishing Company

BIG MATH IDEAS THIS MONTH

Examine two-dimensional shapes, use doubles and doubles plus one facts, identify odd and even, add and subtract mentally, explain place value, regroup to add, estimate, interpret graphs, predict probability

Every Day Calendar

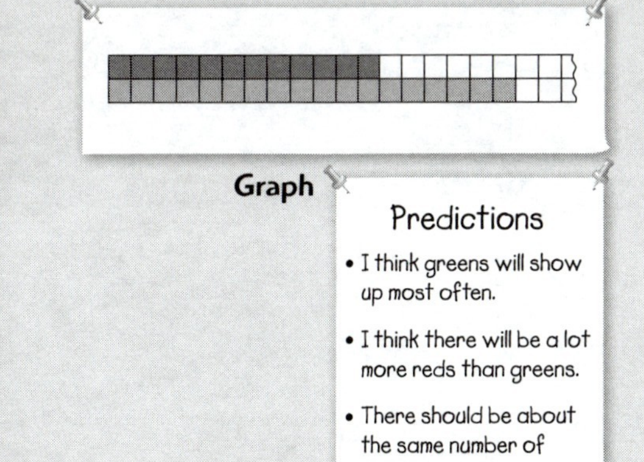

Graph

Predictions

- I think greens will show up most often.
- I think there will be a lot more reds than greens.
- There should be about the same number of reds and greens.

					2	1
					$ $	$
millions	hundred thousands	ten thousands	thousands	hundreds	tens	ones

Daily Depositor

Depositor Record

Day 4: 6 + 4 = 10

Day 5: 10 + 5 = 15

Day 6: 15 + 6 = 21

Computations and Connections Record

$8 + 7 = 15 \qquad 7 + 8 = 15 \qquad 15 - 7 = 8 \qquad 15 - 8 = 7$

$7 + 7 + 1 = 15$

Computations and Connections

1 2 3 4 5 6

Counting Tape

© Houghton Mifflin Harcourt Publishing Company

Monthly Resources

Intervention

- **Odd and Even Numbers: Small Group:** For students who are struggling with odd and even numbers, use counters or other objects, to show that even numbers can be put into groups of 2 without any extras, and odd numbers can be put into groups of 2, but will always have one extra. Allow students to group from 3 to 30 counters to prove whether a number is even or odd. Clarify for students that odd and even numbers can both be counted by 2 as each number is two away from the previous one in its group. (e.g., 1, 3, 5, 7, . . . illustrates skip counting by 2, but the counting sequence started with 1 instead of 0.)

1 2 3 4 5 6 7 8 9 10 11 12 13 14 15 16 17 18

- **Multiples of 5 and 10: Small Group:** Many students can recite a skip counting sequence by 5 and by 10, but may not realize that they are counting by a quantity of 5 or 10. Explain multiples as numbers that can be grouped by the given number or separated into groups of the given number. Use counters to prove that the number 5 is a multiple of 5 because it can be put into a single group of 5 or separated into 5 equal groups (likewise with 10 and any other multiple). Use the self-stick notes on the Counting Tape to show groups of 5 and 10.

- **Multiples on the Calendar: Small Group:** The Calendar shows a pattern of multiples of 2 (AB shape pattern) and an overlapping pattern of multiples of 3 (yellow dot on every third piece). Remove the pieces from the Calendar and place them in a linear fashion. Use counters to show that some multiples of 3 are odd and some are even. Show that the even multiples of 3 are also multiples of 2. Have students explore the quantities and prove whether each number is a multiple of 2, a multiple of 3 or a multiple of both.

More Helpful Hints

- Calendar: At the beginning of the month, put all your Calendar Pieces on the Calendar facing down. This allows for easy access to the appropriate Calendar Piece when students answer a question. (e.g. When asking for the date and shape represented on the third Thursday of the month, the Calendar Piece is in place and only needs to be turned over to check for the correct answer.) It is also a guarantee that all the month's Calendar Pieces are there.

- Depositor: Although it is recommended that the Calendar take only 10–15 minutes of your class time each day, for the end of the month estimation activity to be successful, you will need at least 20–30 minutes. It is important to give students the opportunity to really think about the amount being collected and make their estimations.

- Computations and Collections: Use rings and the student made picture records to create a classroom booklet of the "doubles" and "doubles plus/minus 1" facts. Provide copies of blank Double Ten Grids for each student to make flash cards for the "doubles" and "doubles plus 1" facts.

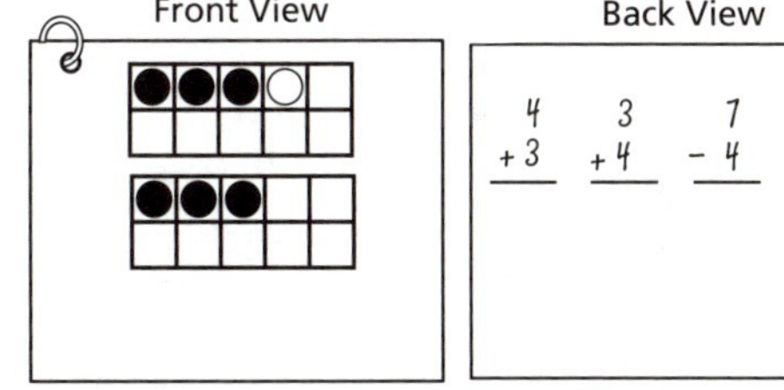

Flash cards for addition and subtraction facts

Assessments

August/September Assessment: See pages 73–76.

Pretest: See pages 57–60.

Addition Facts Progress Record: See page 111.

Assessment Checklist: See pages 109–110.

© Houghton Mifflin Harcourt Publishing Company

August/September Week 1

Vocabulary This Month

Right angles, odd and even numbers, rotate, multiple, estimate, vertex, vertices, probability

Update Questions

Be sure to ask: **What number? Odd or even? What multiple? What amount? What date? What shape? Double or double plus one? What color?**

Elements for Number of Days in School

- Counting Tape and Hundred Chart (TG p. 24 Daily Routine)
- Depositor (TG p. 26 Daily Routine)

Elements for Calendar Date

- Calendar (TG p. 18 Daily Routine)
- Computations and Connections (TG p. 21 Daily Routine)

Extras This Month

- Graph (TG p. 28 Daily Routine)

Discussion Questions

Follow up with these questions: **How did you get your answer? How do these compare or contrast? Explain your reasoning.**

Monday	Tuesday	Wednesday	Thursday	Friday
Calendar (TG p. 19) How would you describe today's Calendar Piece? **Computations and Connections** (TG p. 20) How will today's date be represented on the Double Ten Grids? Can you make a finger pattern that matches? Is this a double or a double plus one?	**Counting Tape and Hundred Chart** (TG p. 24) Is today's number odd or even? Prove your answer. **Depositor** (TG p. 26) Describe the rule for the Depositor. How did you calculate today's total?	**Graph** (TG p. 29) Out of 15 draws, what is your prediction of how many reds will be drawn? Green? What are some other possibilities? **Computations and Connections** (TG p. 20) How will today's date be represented on the ten frames? Is this a double or a double plus one?	**Counting Tape and Hundred Chart** (TG p. 24) What number is circled on the Hundred Chart? Do you say today's number when you count by twos? Explain. **Depositor** (TG p. 26) How much has been collected so far? On what day of school do you think we will reach two hundred dollars?	**Calendar** (TG p. 19) What is the shape pattern? What is the color pattern? **Computations and Connections** (TG p. 20) How will today's date be represented on the Double Ten Grids? Describe the placement of the counters. Is this a double or a double plus one?

TG refers to the Teacher's Guide.

© Houghton Mifflin Harcourt Publishing Company

August/September Week 2

Vocabulary This Month

Right angles, odd and even numbers, rotate, multiple, estimate, vertex, vertices, probability

Update Questions

Be sure to ask: **What number? Odd or even? What multiple? What amount? What date? What shape? Double or double plus one? What color?**

Elements for Number of Days in School

- Counting Tape and Hundred Chart (TG p. 24 Daily Routine)
- Depositor (TG p. 26 Daily Routine)

Elements for Calendar Date

- Calendar (TG p. 18 Daily Routine)
- Computations and Connections (TG p. 21 Daily Routine)

Extras This Month

- Graph (TG p. 28 Daily Routine)

Discussion Questions

Follow up with these questions: **Which strategy did you use? What is the relationship between *a* and *b*? Explain your reasoning.**

Monday	Tuesday	Wednesday	Thursday	Friday
Calendar (TG p. 19) Describe the square piece. What do you observe about the squares? What do you think tomorrow's Calendar Piece will be? Why do you think so? **Computations and Connections** (TG p. 21) What is today's date? How many counters should be represented in the Double Ten Grids? Is this a double or a double plus one? When do you think we will see the next double or double plus one?	**Counting Tape and Hundred Chart** (TG p. 24) What day of school will it be in 10 more school days? In 20 more days? How did you find your answer? Did anyone find the answer a different way? **Depositor** (TG p. 27) How do you know when to trade for a ten dollar bill? How do you know when to trade for a one hundred dollar bill? Will there be any trading for larger bills this week? Explain.	**Graph** (TG p. 29) After today's draw, what is the difference between the number of red and green draws? At the end of the experiment, is it likely that red will be drawn more often? Why or why not?	**Counting Tape and Hundred Chart** (TG p. 24) Will Day 25 will be odd or even? How do you know? How could you use counters to prove if a number is odd or even? **Depositor** (TG p. 27) What is today's total? How many ten dollar bills are in today's amount? How many one dollar bills?	**Calendar** (TG p. 19) How would you describe next Monday's Calendar Piece? How did you choose the Calendar Piece for Monday? **Computations and Connections** (TG p. 22) How will you represent today's amount in the Double Ten Grids? What addition and subtraction facts can you write?

TG refers to the Teacher's Guide.

© Houghton Mifflin Harcourt Publishing Company

August/September Week 3

Vocabulary This Month

Right angles, odd and even numbers, rotate, multiple, estimate, vertex, vertices, probability

Update Questions

Be sure to ask: **What number? Odd or even? What multiple? What amount? What date? What shape? Double or double plus one? What color?**

Elements for Number of Days in School

- Counting Tape and Hundred Chart (TG p. 24 Daily Routine)
- Depositor (TG p. 26 Daily Routine)

Elements for Calendar Date

- Calendar (TG p. 18 Daily Routine)
- Computations and Connections (TG p. 21 Daily Routine)

Extras This Month

- Graph (TG p. 28 Daily Routine)

Discussion Questions

Follow up with these questions: **How did you get your answer? What is the relationship between *a* and *b*? How do these compare or contrast? Explain your reasoning.**

Monday	Tuesday	Wednesday	Thursday	Friday
Calendar (TG p. 19) What do you notice about the yellow dots? **Computations and Connections** (TG p. 22) Describe the number of counters in today's Double Ten Grids. What addition and subtraction facts can we write? What stories might go with these number sentences?	**Counting Tape and Hundred Chart** (TG p. 25) How many more days until we are in school 30 days? How did you get your answer? **Depositor** (TG p. 27) How much money is in the Depositor so far? What is the value of each digit in the number?	**Graph** (TG p. 29) After today's draw, what color has been drawn the most so far? By the end of the experiment, do you think the red and green will be drawn the same number of times? Explain your thinking.	**Counting Tape and Hundred Chart** (TG p. 25) How many even days are shown on the Counting Tape so far? How many odd days? **Depositor** (TG p. 27) Explain how you would use mental math to add \$13 to \$78. What is the sum?	**Calendar** (TG p. 19) What is the number relationship between the Calendar Pieces with yellow dots and circles and the pieces with yellow dots and squares? Explain. **Computations and Connections** (TG p. 22) Describe the number of counters in today's Double Ten Grids. What number stories might go with this description?

TG refers to the Teacher's Guide.

© Houghton Mifflin Harcourt Publishing Company

August/September Week 4

Vocabulary This Month

Right angles, odd and even numbers, rotate, multiple, estimate, vertex, vertices, probability

Update Questions

Be sure to ask: **What number? Odd or even? What multiple? What amount? What date? What shape? Double or double plus one? What color?**

Elements for Number of Days in School

- Counting Tape and Hundred Chart (TG p. 24 Daily Routine)
- Depositor (TG p. 26 Daily Routine)

Elements for Calendar Date

- Calendar (TG p. 18 Daily Routine)
- Computations and Connections (TG p. 21 Daily Routine)

Extras This Month

- Graph (TG p. 28 Daily Routine)

Discussion Questions

Follow up with these questions: **How do you know? How did you get your answer? How do these compare or contrast? Explain your reasoning.**

Monday	Tuesday	Wednesday	Thursday	Friday
Calendar (TG p. 19) How many right angles are in today's Calendar Piece? **Computations and Connections** (TG p. 22) Write several addition facts on the board. Which one of these facts is a double? What is the sum?	**Counting Tape and Hundred Chart** (TG p. 25) How can we express today's number in tens and ones? **Depositor** (TG p. 27) How would you count today's total by tens and ones?	**Calendar** (TG p. 19) What do you notice about all the corners/vertices of the square? **Graph** (TG p. 29) How do the results of the experiment compare with our predictions? If we did the experiment again, do you think the results would be different? Why?	**Counting Tape and Hundred Chart** (TG p. 25) How many more days until we are in school 40 days? How did you get your answer? **Depositor** (TG p. 27) If there are 180 school days, what is your estimate of how much money will be collected by the end of the school year? Explain.	**Calendar** (TG p. 19) How many of this month's Calendar Pieces are circles? How many are squares? How many Calendar Pieces are multiples of 3? **Computations and Connections** (TG p. 22) Write several addition facts. Which of these facts is a double plus one? What doubles fact helps you figure that out?

TG refers to the Teacher's Guide.

© Houghton Mifflin Harcourt Publishing Company

Big Math Ideas This Month

Examine two types of triangles, explore 10+ addition facts, measure length in metric units, understand A.M. and P.M., tell time to the hour, explain place value, count mixed coins, collect and display weather data in a bar graph

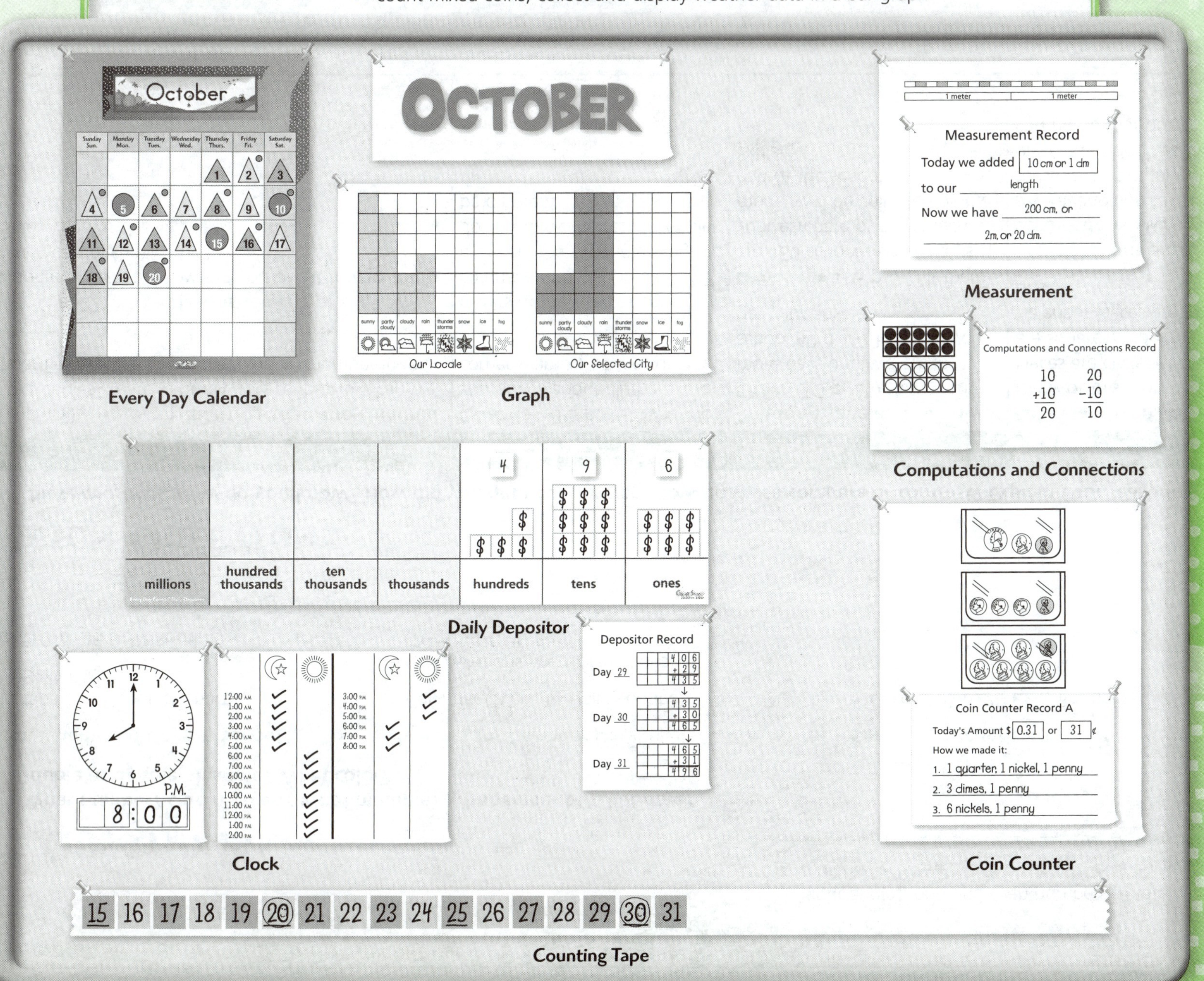

© Houghton Mifflin Harcourt Publishing Company

Monthly Resources

Intervention

- **Multiples of 2, 5 and 10: Small Group:** This month, students will look at grouping the day's number on the Counting Tape by 2s, 5s, or 10s. While they may be able to count by 2s, 5s, or 10s, they may not realize that the day's number could be a multiple of one of these numbers. Review multiples as numbers that can be grouped by the given number or separated into groups of the given number. Use counters or the self-stick notes from the Counting Tape to check whether a given number is a multiple of 2, 5, or 10.
- **Difference Between Two Numbers: Small Group:** For students struggling with the mental math questions about the difference between the day's number and 100, begin with questions about the difference between the day's number and the next ten. Then ask questions about the difference between the day's number and the next 2 tens and so on. For example on Day 36, ask the difference between 36 and 40. Then ask the difference between 36 and 50. Ask the student to explain how he figured out the answer. Continue asking the difference between the day's number and the next greater ten until the number 100 has been reached. This same strategy can be helpful to obtain the total in the Depositor as well, since adding the day's amount is to be done mentally. Counting by 10s off the decade (e.g. 17, 27, 37, , , ,) can also be helpful.

More Helpful Hints

- Graph: At the end of the month, put the two graphs aside. You will need them in January, when graphs will be made for winter forecasts in the same two locations.
- Coin Counter: While *Calendar Math* provides play money cardstock and demonstration coins to place on the board, some teachers like to use real money or plastic money for the students to manipulate during discussions. Cutting egg cartons into thirds provides a container for each student. Each student will have storage for quarters, dimes, nickels and pennies; and four to eight containers stack nicely for storage.
- Measurement: Have students cut the 10 cm by 5 cm strips in advance and add one strip to the Measurement display in the classroom throughout the month. On days used to discuss Measurement, refer to the total that the students have mounted to match the day of the month.

1 meter = 10 decimeters = 100 centimeters

Assessments

October Assessment: See pages 77–80.

Addition Facts Progress Record: See page 111.

Assessment Checklist: See pages 109–110.

© Houghton Mifflin Harcourt Publishing Company

October Week 1

Vocabulary This Month

Equilateral triangle, isosceles triangle, A.M. and P.M., centimeter, decimeter, meter

Update Questions

Be sure to ask: **What number? Is it odd or even? What multiple? What amount? How many since? How long ago? What date? What shape? What color? What time?**

Elements for Number of Days in School

- Counting Tape and Hundred Chart (TG p. 39 Daily Routine)
- Depositor (TG p. 41 Daily Routine)
- Coin Counter (TG p. 42 Daily Routine)

Elements for Calendar Date

- Calendar (TG p. 32 Daily Routine)
- Computations and Connections (TG p. 34 Daily Routine)

Extras This Month

- Graph (TG p. 44 Daily Routine)
- Measurement (TG p. 36 Daily Routine)
- Clock (TG p. 38 Daily Routine)

Discussion Questions

Follow up with these questions: **How do you know? How did you get your answer? How do these compare or contrast? What is the relationship between *a* and *b*? Explain your reasoning.**

Monday	Tuesday	Wednesday	Thursday	Friday
Calendar (TG p. 32) How would you describe today's Calendar Piece? **Measurement** (TG p. 36) On what day will we reach one meter? How many centimeters are in one meter? **Clock** (TG p. 38) What time is shown on the clock? Is it A.M. or P.M.? Is it dark or light outside?	**Counting Tape and Hundred Chart** (TG p. 39) Is today's number odd or even? How many days has it been since the 12th day of school? **Depositor** (TG p. 41) How much will be added to the Depositor today? How did you find the total? Does anyone have a different way?	**Graph** (TG p. 44) How are we recording temperature this month? How will we determine how to color 82 degrees? 67 degrees? **Counting Tape and Hundred Chart** (TG p. 40) Explain why 6 has two Multiple Markers, one for 2 and one for 3. What are some other numbers that will have both a heart and a triangle? Why?	**Counting Tape and Hundred Chart** (TG p. 39) Tell a multiples of 2 story. Write the story, draw a picture and write the number sentence. **Clock** (TG p. 43) How can you estimate the time without seeing the clock up close?	**Calendar** (TG p. 32) Describe the difference triangles on the Calendar Pieces. **Coin Counter** (TG p. 42) How can you make 23¢ with 5 coins? **Computations and Connections** (TG p. 34) What number sentences describe today's Double Ten Grid?

TG refers to the Teacher's Guide.

© Houghton Mifflin Harcourt Publishing Company

October Week 2

Vocabulary This Month

Equilateral triangle, isosceles triangle, A.M. and P.M., centimeter, decimeter, meter

Update Questions

Be sure to ask: **What number? Is it odd or even? What multiple? What amount? How many since? How long ago? What date? What shape? What color? What time?**

Elements for Number of Days in School

- Counting Tape and Hundred Chart (TG p. 39 Daily Routine)
- Depositor (TG p. 41 Daily Routine)
- Coin Counter (TG p. 42 Daily Routine)

Elements for Calendar Date

- Calendar (TG p. 32 Daily Routine)
- Computations and Connections (TG p. 34 Daily Routine)

Extras This Month

- Graph (TG p. 44 Daily Routine)
- Measurement (TG p. 36 Daily Routine)
- Clock (TG p. 38 Daily Routine)

Discussion Questions

Follow up with these questions: **How do you know? How did you get your answer? How do these compare or contrast? Explain your reasoning.**

Monday	Tuesday	Wednesday	Thursday	Friday
Calendar (TG p. 32) How would you describe the numbers that have red dots on them? **Measurement** (TG p. 36) How many days until we reach the next meter? **Clock** (TG p. 38) Describe how the clock looks. How is this time written in digital form?	**Counting Tape and Hundred Chart** (TG p. 40) What numbers on the Counting Tape are multiples of 5? **Depositor** (TG p. 41) How many more school days until we collect our next $100 bill? **Coin Counter** (TG p. 42) What is the greatest number of nickels you could use to make 41¢? How did you get your answer?	**Graph** (TG p. 45) How many sunny days in our city have we graphed so far this month? Cloudy days? **Computations and Connections** (TG p. 34) How many of sections of the ten grid are filled today? Empty? Can you tell me an addition story about these two numbers? **Clock** (TG p. 38) What time was it 3 hours ago? What could you have been doing at that time?	**Counting Tape and Hundred Chart** (TG p. 40) How many more days until the 50th day? The 100th day? **Depositor** (TG p. 41) Look at today's total. What is the value of the digit in the hundreds place? **Coin Counter** (TG p. 44) How much money would you have left today if you spent 10¢? 15¢?	**Calendar** (TG p. 32) If the pattern continues, what shape will be on the third Sunday? **Computations and Connections** (TG p. 35) Describe the Ten Grid(s). Can you tell a subtraction story to match the Double Ten Grid? **Measurement** (TG p. 35) Would you use centimeters or meters to measure the size of a piece of paper?

TG refers to the Teacher's Guide.

© Houghton Mifflin Harcourt Publishing Company

October Week 3

Vocabulary This Month

Equilateral triangle, isosceles triangle, A.M. and P.M., centimeter, decimeter, meter

Update Questions

Be sure to ask: **What number? Is it odd or even? What multiple? What amount? How many since? How long ago? What date? What shape? What color? What time?**

Elements for Number of Days in School

- Counting Tape and Hundred Chart (TG p. 39 Daily Routine)
- Depositor (TG p. 41 Daily Routine)
- Coin Counter (TG p. 42 Daily Routine)

Elements for Calendar Date

- Calendar (TG p. 32 Daily Routine)
- Computations and Connections (TG p. 34 Daily Routine)

Extras This Month

- Graph (TG p. 44 Daily Routine)
- Measurement (TG p. 36 Daily Routine)
- Clock (TG p. 38 Daily Routine)

Discussion Questions

Follow up with these questions: **How do you know? How did you get your answer? How do these compare or contrast? Explain your reasoning.**

Monday	Tuesday	Wednesday	Thursday	Friday
Calendar (TG p. 32) What numbers are on the orange triangles? Describe the pattern of these numbers. **Measurement** (TG p. 35) How many decimeters are in 2 meters? How many centimeters are in 2 meters? **Clock** (TG p. 38) What time does the clock show? What time did the clock change from A.M. to P.M.?	**Counting Tape and Hundred Chart** (TG p. 40) Count to today's number by 5s. Are there any extras? **Depositor** (TG p. 41) How could you make today's amount using hundred dollar, ten dollar and one dollar bills? Make a list. **Coin Counter** (TG p. 43) How much money would I get if I shared today's amount with a friend? Is there any money left over?	**Graph** (TG p. 45) In our sample, how many more days has the weather forecast at home been sunny (or cloudy) than the weather forecast in our selected city? **Computations and Connections** (TG p. 35) What 10 plus fact is represented today? What are the two addends? How many fives are in your number?	**Counting Tape and Hundred Chart** (TG p. 40) How many days have passed since Day 13? Since Day 25? **Depositor** (TG p. 41) How would you add 351 + 27? What about 378 + 28? **Coin Counter** (TG p. 44) How much more money do you need to get $0.50? $1.00?	**Calendar** (TG p. 32) What is the difference between today's date and the last day of the month? **Computations and Connections** (TG p. 35) Write all possible number sentences to describe what is shown in today's Double Ten Grid(s). **Measurement** (TG p. 37) Where do you think the strips will reach by the end of the month? Estimate.

TG refers to the Teacher's Guide.

© Houghton Mifflin Harcourt Publishing Company

October Week 4

Vocabulary This Month

Equilateral triangle, isosceles triangle, A.M. and P.M., centimeter, decimeter, meter

Update Questions

***Be sure to ask:* What number? Is it odd or even? What multiple? What amount? How many since? How long ago? What date? What shape? What color? What time?**

Elements for Number of Days in School

- Counting Tape and Hundred Chart (TG p. 39 Daily Routine)
- Depositor (TG p. 41 Daily Routine)
- Coin Counter (TG p. 42 Daily Routine)

Elements for Calendar Date

- Calendar (TG p. 32 Daily Routine)
- Computations and Connections (TG p. 34 Daily Routine)

Extras This Month

- Graph (TG p. 44 Daily Routine)
- Measurement (TG p. 36 Daily Routine)
- Clock (TG p. 38 Daily Routine)

Discussion Questions

***Follow up with these questions:* How do you know? How did you get your answer? How do these compare or contrast? Explain your reasoning.**

Monday	Tuesday	Wednesday	Thursday	Friday
Calendar (TG p. 33) How many of this month's pieces are equilateral triangles? Isosceles triangles? Circles? List the attributes of each. **Measurement** (TG p. 37) How many whole meters are there? How many extra centimeters? **Clock** (TG p. 38) If it is 9 o'clock and school started an hour ago, what time did school start? Is that A.M. or P.M.?	**Counting Tape and Hundred Chart** (TG p. 40) Choose any two odd numbers on the tape and add them together. What type of number do you have now? Explain. **Depositor** (TG p. 42) What are two different strategies you could use to find today's total? **Coin Counter** (TG p. 43) If you doubled today's amount, how much would you have?	**Graph** (TG p. 45) How many rainy days need to be forecast at home to catch up to the rainy days forecast in the selected city? **Computations and Connections** (TG p. 35) Write an addition sentence on the board. Which ten grid record matches the number sentence? Can you write another?	**Counting Tape and Hundred Chart** (TG p. 40) If Team A scores 31 points in the first quarter and Team B scores 19 points, how many points behind is Team B? **Depositor** (TG p. 42) Have you changed your estimate for how much money you think we will collect by the end of the year? Explain. **Coin Counter** (TG p. 44) How much money will you have in 10 more days? 15 more days?	**Calendar** (TG p. 33) What three-dimensional shape has a triangle for a face? **Computations and Connections** (TG p. 35) How does understanding 10 + 3 help you understand 20 + 3? 30 + 3? 70 + 3? **Clock** (TG p. 38) How many times in a 24 hour period does the clock read 6:00? How many hours are in a day?

TG refers to the Teacher's Guide.

© Houghton Mifflin Harcourt Publishing Company

Big Math Ideas This Month

Examine a rhombus, square, and rectangle; use "Make a Fast 10" strategy with 9+ facts; measure length in inches, feet, and yards; tell time to the minute; round to the nearest ten; add and subtract mentally; identify coordinates on a graph

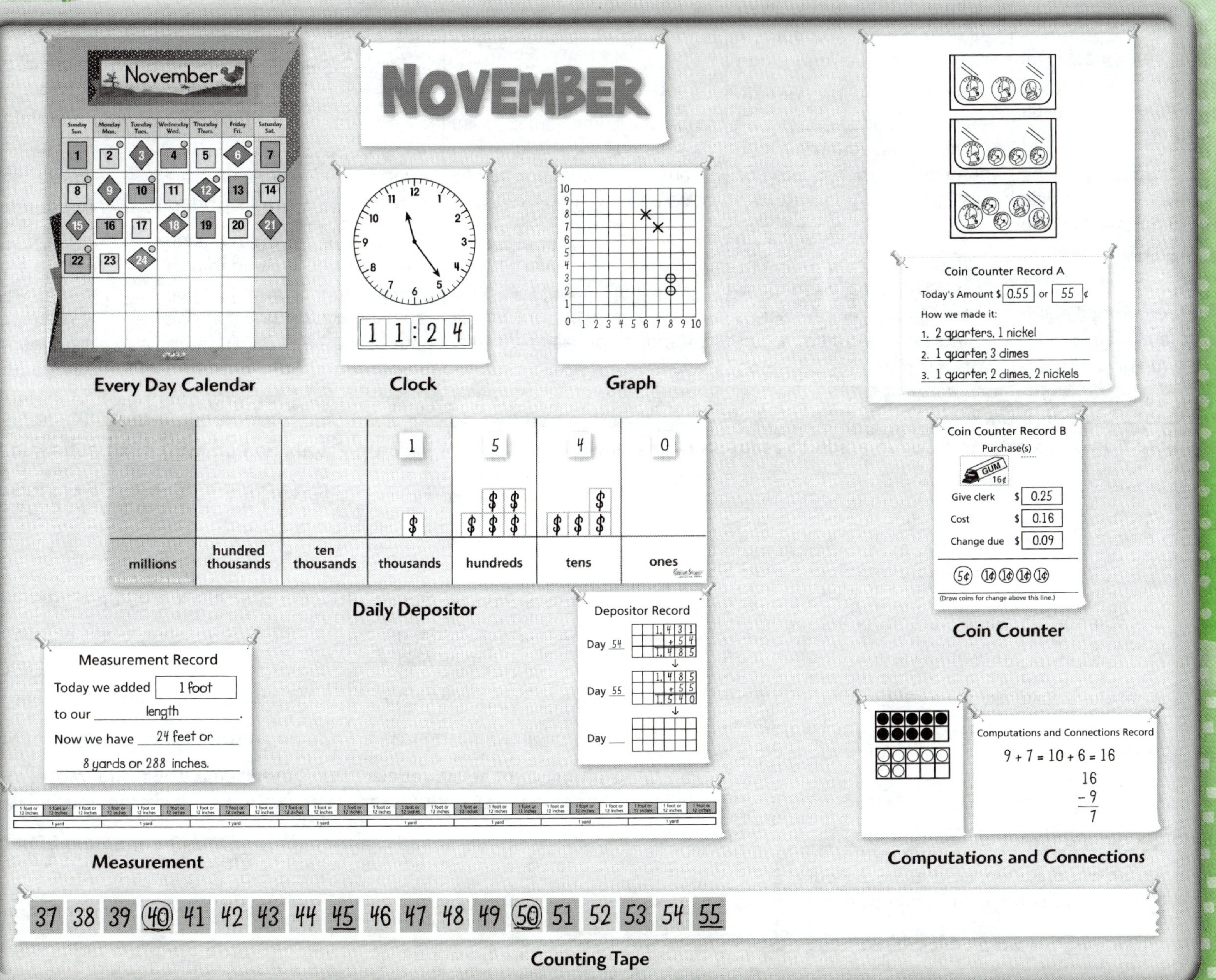

© Houghton Mifflin Harcourt Publishing Company

Monthly Resources

Intervention

- **Rounding to the Nearest Ten: Small Group:** The Counting Tape is an excellent model to develop conceptual understanding of rounding numbers to the nearest ten. Begin by choosing a number for the students to round. Lift the self-stick note with that number and place it above the tape in its same spot. Then ask which 2 tens it falls between. Lift the self-stick notes with the 2 tens on them above the Counting Tape in their same spots. This creates an excellent visual for the ten in which the given number is closest. Have students describe the given number's placement in relation to the 2 tens. Then ask, "To which ten should we round the given number?" Initially, avoid numbers with 5 ones as developing a rounding rule for these numbers is difficult to explain without using a real-life estimation example.

- **Make a Fast Ten Strategy: Small Group:** When reviewing the "Make a Fast 10" strategy with 9 plus facts, some students may not "see" the ten that is being created. Using blank Double Ten Grids (TR2) with counters can be helpful. Have students create the 9 plus number sentence with counters on the two Ten Grids. Then have students move the last counter from the bottom Ten Grid (second addend) up to the top Ten Grid to transform the 9 plus number sentence to a 10 plus number sentence. Remind students that they learned the 10 plus facts the previous month and can use what they know to help with 9 plus, 8 plus and 7 plus facts if they can visualize the ten they are creating.

"Moving 1 up makes a Fast Ten. Then add the rest. So 9 + 6 is the same as 10 + 5, or 15."

More Helpful Hints

- Computations and Connections: To help students learn all the facts to 18, give them copies of Double Ten Grids (TR2) to make cards illustrating facts they need to practice. Students can use these cards with a partner to tell their strategies and state an addition and subtraction fact to go with each card.

- Measurement: Some teachers use this opportunity to introduce or review fractions with thirds by labeling each foot $\frac{1}{3}$ of a yard. To do this, first post the yard strip so students can visualize 1 foot as a *third of a yard*. Then each time a foot is added to the length, another third is added. This can also be used to show the addition of fractions with like denominators.

You can introduce or review fractions with this activity.

- Depositor: Play *I Am Thinking of a Number*. Example: "I am thinking of a number that has 3 hundreds, 7 tens, and 8 ones. What is my number?" To increase the difficulty, play with just tens and ones. Example: "I am thinking of a number that has 49 tens, and 6 ones. What is my number?"

- Graph: You can tailor this activity to your students' needs. To start at a simpler level, use a 4 by 4 grid, or have each team try to get 3 marks in a row. The grid can grow during the month, as can the number of marks in a line needed to win.

Assessments

November Assessment: See pages 81–84.

Addition Facts Progress Record: See page 111.

Assessment Checklist: See pages 109–110.

© Houghton Mifflin Harcourt Publishing Company

November Week 1

Vocabulary This Month

Rhombus, rotating, rounding, expanded notation, quarter past the hour, half past the hour, feet, yard, coordinate graph

Update Questions

Be sure to ask: **What number? Is the number odd or even? What multiple? What is the amount? How many since? How long ago? What date? What shape? What color? What time?**

Elements for Number of Days in School

- Counting Tape and Hundred Chart (TG p. 55 Daily Routine)
- Depositor (TG p. 57 Daily Routine)
- Coin Counter (TG p. 59)

Elements for Calendar Date

- Calendar (TG p. 48 Daily Routine)
- Computations and Connections (TG p. 50 Daily Routine)
- Clock (TG p. 53 Daily Routine)

Extras This Month

- Graph (TG p. 60 Daily Routine)
- Measurement (TG p. 52 Daily Routine)

Discussion Questions

Follow up with these questions: **How do you know? How did you get your answer? How do these compare or contrast? Explain your reasoning.**

Monday	Tuesday	Wednesday	Thursday	Friday
Calendar (TG p. 48) How would you describe the Calendar Pieces so far? **Measurement** (TG p. 52) How many strips were posted today? How many feet is that? How many inches? **Clock** (TG p. 54) What time does the Clock read now? How many minutes after the hour is that?	**Counting Tape and Hundred Chart** (TG p. 55) How many even numbers have appeared on the tape so far? Prove that one of them is even. **Depositor** (TG p. 57) What is your estimate of the amount in the Depositor on the 50th day of school? **Coin Counter** (TG p. 58) Name two combinations of coins that have a value of 47¢.	**Graph** (TG p. 60) On a coordinate graph, which is the *x*-axis and which is the *y*-axis? How do you plot a point on a coordinate graph? **Computations and Connections** (TG p. 50) What number sentence could you write to describe the counters and empty spaces in the Ten Grid? **Clock** (TG p. 54) Draw what a clock looks like at 11:07.	**Counting Tape and Hundred Chart** (TG p. 55) How many groups of 5 are in 30? In 42? How did you get your answers? **Depositor** (TG p. 57) What is today's number written in expanded notation? In words? **Coin Counter** (TG p. 59) A pencil costs 28¢. You give the clerk 50¢. What change will you receive?	**Calendar** (TG p. 48) What Calendar Piece will appear a week from now? How do you know? Share another reason. **Computations and Connections** (TG p. 50) List the combinations for 10 that you have reviewed so far. Can you tell a number story to go with one of them? **Measurement** (TG p. 52) How many inches are in 2 feet? In 4 feet? In 6 feet?

TG refers to the Teacher's Guide.

© Houghton Mifflin Harcourt Publishing Company

November Week 2

Vocabulary This Month

Rhombus, rotating, rounding, expanded notation, quarter past the hour, half past the hour, feet, yard, coordinate graph

Update Questions

Be sure to ask: **What number? Is the number odd or even? What multiple? What is the amount? How many since? How long ago? What date? What shape? What color? What time?**

Elements for Number of Days in School

- Counting Tape and Hundred Chart (TG p. 55 Daily Routine)
- Depositor (TG p. 57 Daily Routine)
- Coin Counter (TG p. 59)

Elements for Calendar Date

- Calendar (TG p. 48 Daily Routine)
- Computations and Connections (TG p. 50 Daily Routine)
- Clock (TG p. 53 Daily Routine)

Extras This Month

- Graph (TG p. 60 Daily Routine)
- Measurement (TG p. 52 Daily Routine)

Discussion Questions

Follow up with these questions: **How do you know? How did you get your answer? How do these compare or contrast? Explain your reasoning.**

Monday	Tuesday	Wednesday	Thursday	Friday
Calendar (TG p. 48) What do you notice about the rectangles? The rhombuses? Do the squares seem to follow the same rotating pattern?	**Counting Tape and Hundred Chart** (TG p. 56) If you have 43 apples, how many more do you need to make 100 apples? How did you get your answer? Explain.	**Graph** (TG p. 61) I have plotted 4 points on the Graph. Tell me the coordinates for these points.	**Counting Tape and Hundred Chart** (TG p. 56) Which tens does today's number fall between? Which ten is it closer to? How do we round today's number to the nearest ten?	**Calendar** (TG p. 48) Describe the number pattern that will appear on Mondays. Why does this occur?
Measurement (TG p. 52) How many days until we reach our next full yard? How many yards will that be in all?	**Depositor** (TG p. 57) Is today's total closer to $1,100 or $1,200? How could you find out?	**Computations and Connections** (TG p. 50) Write all possible number sentences to describe what is shown on the Ten Grid(s).	**Depositor** (TG p. 57) What is the value of the digit 0 in 1,081? What would happen if the zero wasn't there?	**Computations and Connections** (TG p. 50) How does making a fast 10 help you add today's 9 plus fact?
Clock (TG p. 54) How many more minutes until it is a quarter after 11? What is another way to read that time?	**Coin Counter** (TG p. 59) How can we show 47¢ with the least number of coins? Show another combination using 6 coins.	**Clock** (TG p. 54) If the time is 11:18, about where will the minute hand be? Will it be closest to the 2, the 3, or the 4? Why?	**Coin Counter** (TG p. 59) Milk at lunch costs 50¢. You have 36¢. How much more money do you need?	**Measurement** (TG p. 52) How long is our total length in feet? How many yards is that? How many extra feet?

TG refers to the Teacher's Guide.

© Houghton Mifflin Harcourt Publishing Company

November Week 3

Vocabulary This Month

Rhombus, rotating, rounding, expanded notation, quarter past the hour, half past the hour, feet, yard, coordinate graph

Update Questions

***Be sure to ask:* What number? Is the number odd or even? What multiple? What is the amount? How many since? How long ago? What date? What shape? What color? What time?**

Elements for Number of Days in School

- Counting Tape and Hundred Chart (TG p. 55 Daily Routine)
- Depositor (TG p. 57 Daily Routine)
- Coin Counter (TG p. 59)

Elements for Calendar Date

- Calendar (TG p. 48 Daily Routine)
- Computations and Connections (TG p. 50 Daily Routine)
- Clock (TG p. 53 Daily Routine)

Extras This Month

- Graph (TG p. 60 Daily Routine)
- Measurement (TG p. 52 Daily Routine)

Discussion Questions

***Follow up with these questions:* How do you know? How did you get your answer? How do these compare or contrast? Explain your reasoning.**

Monday	Tuesday	Wednesday	Thursday	Friday
Calendar (TG p. 48) Describe the shape pattern of the Calendar Pieces with green dots. What types of numerals do not have green dots? **Measurement** (TG p. 51) How many yards are in 10 feet? How did you figure that out? **Clock** (TG p. 54) Where will the hour hand be on the last day of November? Why will it be in that position?	**Counting Tape and Hundred Chart** (TG p. 56) What is today's number plus 10? Minus 10? **Depositor** (TG p. 57) What is today's number written in expanded notation? In words? How many hundreds are there? Tens? **Coin Counter** (TG p. 59) Which of today's coin(s) would you use to buy a 16¢ pack of gum? How much change would you receive?	**Graph** (TG p. 61) Team A has marked the coordinate (3, 2). What is one coordinate that could block their attempt to get four in a row? **Computations and Connections** (TG p. 49) How would you use mental math to add 9 + 8? **Clock** (TG p. 54) What is another way to read the Clock at 15 minutes after the hour? At 30 minutes after the hour?	**Counting Tape and Hundred Chart** (TG p. 56) How many days have we been in school since Day 25? **Depositor** (TG p. 58) If we had to buy \$95 worth of groceries with today's amount, how much would we have left? Explain your answer. **Coin Counter** (TG p. 59) With a partner, make a list of 5 combinations for 50¢. Share your list with the class.	**Calendar** (TG p. 48) What is the distance between rectangles with green dots? Why do you think this occurs? **Computations and Connections** (TG p. 50) Which 10 plus fact from October could help you solve today's 9 plus fact? What is the relationship? **Measurement** (TG p. 52) How many desks could you line up to equal the length of our strips?

TG refers to the Teacher's Guide.

© Houghton Mifflin Harcourt Publishing Company

November Week 4

Vocabulary This Month

Rhombus, rotating, rounding, expanded notation, quarter past the hour, half past the hour, feet, yard, coordinate graph

Update Questions

Be sure to ask: **What number? Is the number odd or even? What multiple? What is the amount? How many since? How long ago? What date? What shape? What color? What time?**

Elements for Number of Days in School

- Counting Tape and Hundred Chart (TG p. 55 Daily Routine)
- Depositor (TG p. 57 Daily Routine)
- Coin Counter (TG p. 59)

Elements for Calendar Date

- Calendar (TG p. 48 Daily Routine)
- Computations and Connections (TG p. 50 Daily Routine)
- Clock (TG p. 53 Daily Routine)

Extras This Month

- Graph (TG p. 60 Daily Routine)
- Measurement (TG p. 52 Daily Routine)

Discussion Questions

Follow up with these questions: **How do you know? How did you get your answer? How do these compare or contrast? Explain your reasoning.**

Monday	Tuesday	Wednesday	Thursday	Friday
Calendar (TG p. 48) How are the three shapes alike? Different? Does rotation affect the shapes' properties? **Measurement** (TG p. 52) How many yards will we have by the end of the month? Feet? Inches? **Clock** (TG p. 54) If a digital clock says 11:27, how many minutes past the hour is it?	**Counting Tape and Hundred Chart** (TG p. 56) Which tens does today's number fall between? What is today's number rounded to the nearest ten? **Depositor** (TG p. 57) What is the value of the digit in the hundreds place? How many days until we reach the next thousand? **Coin Counter** (TG p. 59) What is today's total in the Coin Counter? How many days until we reach $1.00?	**Graph** (TG p. 61) Did you choose your mark to make a move forward? Or to protect your team? Is there a strategy that ensures you will win? **Computations and Connections** (TG p. 50) Describe how you could use the make a fast 10 strategy with an 8 plus fact. **Clock** (TG p. 54) What time is on the Clock? What time was it 5 minutes ago? Two minutes ago?	**Counting Tape and Hundred Chart** (TG p. 56) Is today's number a multiple of 5? If no, what is the next multiple of 5 that appears? Is that number also a multiple of 2? **Depositor** (TG p. 58) What is today's total? What strategy did you use to add the day's amount? **Coin Counter** (TG p. 59) How will you know if you have today's total using the least amount of coins?	**Counting Tape and Hundred Chart** (TG p. 56) What is the next multiple of 5 that appears? Is that number also a multiple of 2? **Depositor** (TG p. 58) How much money will we add today? What is today's total? What strategy did you use? **Measurement** (TG p. 52) What is our total length in yards, feet and inches?

TG refers to the Teacher's Guide.

© Houghton Mifflin Harcourt Publishing Company

Big Math Ideas This Month

Examine trapezoids, hexagons, and reflections; understand multiplication as adding equal amounts; know minutes in an hour, half hour, and quarter hour; compare numbers; express numbers in expanded notation; make change for a dollar

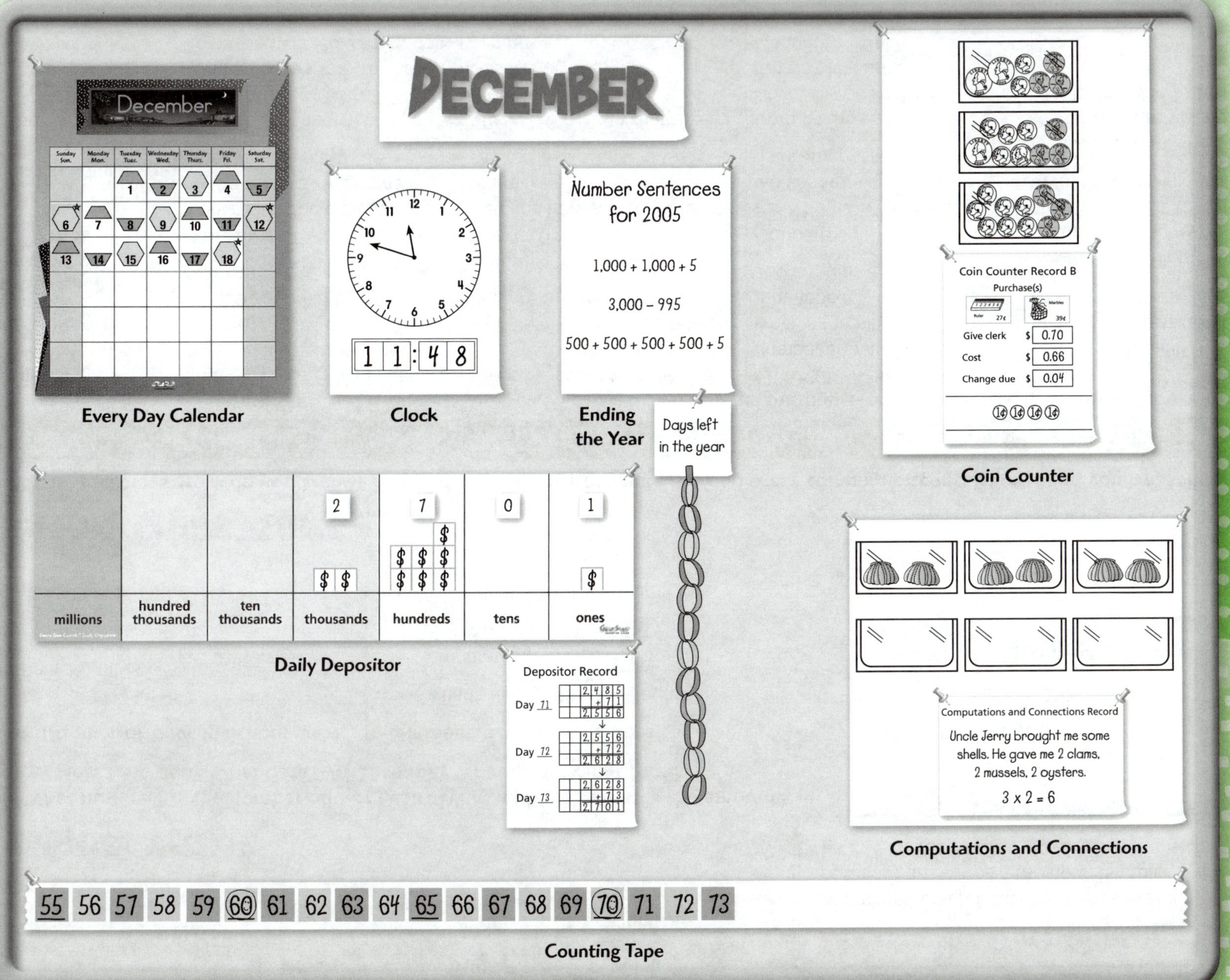

© Houghton Mifflin Harcourt Publishing Company

Monthly Resources

Intervention

- **Multiplication: Small Groups:** If students are having difficulty with creating their own multiplication stories and/or number stories to match them, use small paper plates (or construction paper cut outs) and counters for students to manipulate to act out a given story. Explain that any multiplication or division problem has three parts: the number of groups, the number in each group, and the total. Tell a story and have the students recreate it with the plates and counters. For example, "There are three boys and each of them has 2 basketballs. How many basketballs are there altogether?" Ask, "How many groups are there?" (three), "How many are in each group?" (two basketballs), "How many altogether?" (6 basketballs). Another example, "I have 12 cookies to share. I want to split them among 3 friends. How many cookies will each friend receive?" Ask, "How many groups are there?" (three), "How many are in each group?" (unknown number of cookies), "How many altogether?" (12 cookies). The students share the 12 cookies (counters) among the three friends (plates) to tell how many each friend (plate) received.
- **Comparing Numbers: Small Groups:** Comparing two numbers on the Counting Tape can prove conceptually difficult if students have been taught the trick of only looking at the first number (and subsequent numbers only if necessary) in order to compare. There should be an understanding of the magnitude of number to make the decision about which one is greater. Begin by comparing two consecutive numbers on the Counting Tape by lifting the self-stick notes with those numbers and place them above the tape in their same spots. Have students describe the distance each number is from the beginning of the Counting Tape. Have them decide which number comes after the other if they were counting. Have them build each number with manipulatives. Once they can prove the relationship, have them write and read the comparison with the < and > symbols. Try this with several different numbers on the Counting Tape.

More Helpful Hints

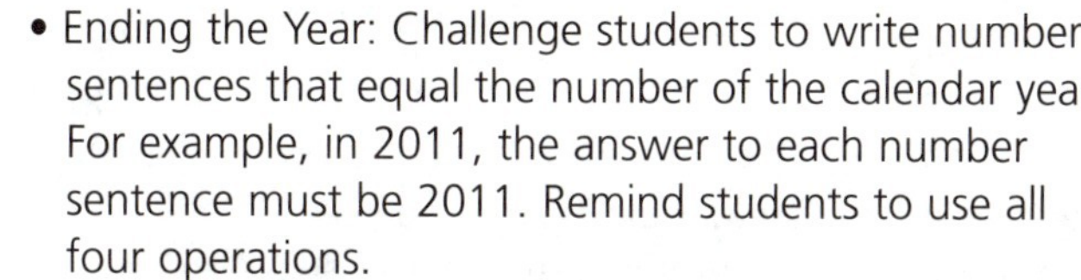

- Ending the Year: Challenge students to write number sentences that equal the number of the calendar year. For example, in 2011, the answer to each number sentence must be 2011. Remind students to use all four operations.
- Calendar: Use the copy of the Calendar Pieces (TR25) for students to explore the relationships between the trapezoid and the hexagon, the relationship between the reflected trapezoid pieces, and congruency between trapezoid pieces (and hexagon pieces).

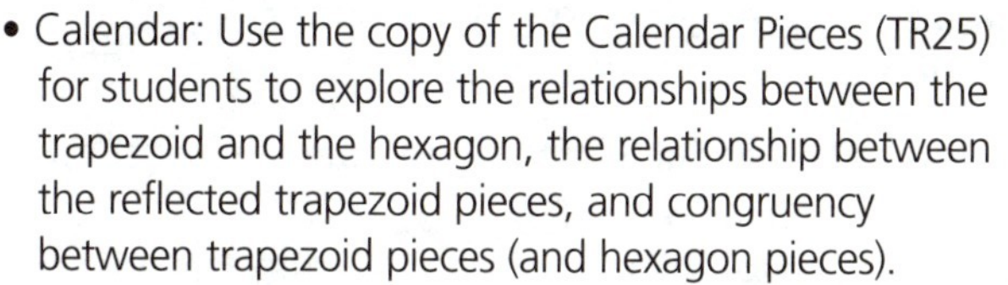

- Clock: To practice reading the time on the clock, students can play a version of *Clock Race*. Each child will need two different color crayons, a copy of the Clock (TR12), and a 1–6 number cube. Players set the time to an hour of their preference and take turns rolling the cube and coloring in that many minutes on the clock, alternating colors with each toss. Before each roll, players state the time on their clocks and the position of the hour hand and minute hand. The first player to color in 30 minutes wins. If time allows, students may continue play to fill in the remaining half of the clock.

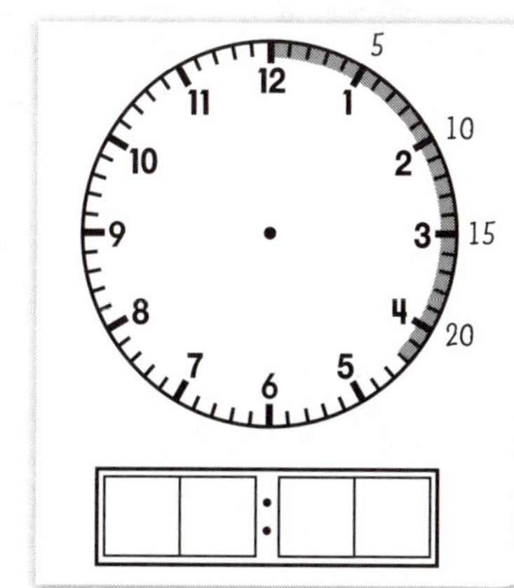

Playing Clock Race: "I have 22 minutes."

Assessments

December Assessment: See pages 85–88.

Winter Test: See pages 61–64.

Multiplication Facts Progress Record: See page 112.

Assessment Checklist: See pages 109–110.

© Houghton Mifflin Harcourt Publishing Company

December Week 1

Vocabulary This Month

Trapezoid, reflection, congruent, less than and greater than symbols (< and >), quarter till the hour

Update Questions

Be sure to ask: **What number? Is the number odd or even? What multiple? What amount? How many since? How long ago? What date? What shape? What color? What time?**

Elements for Number of Days in School

- Counting Tape and Hundred Chart (TG p. 69 Daily Routine)
- Depositor (TG p. 70 Daily Routine)
- Coin Counter (TG p. 71 Daily Routine)

Elements for Calendar Date

- Calendar (TG p. 64 Daily Routine)
- Computations and Connections (TG p. 66 Daily Routine)
- Clock (TG p. 68 Daily Routine)

Extras This Month

- Ending the Year (TG p. 64)

Discussion Questions

Follow up with these questions: **How do you know? How did you get your answer? How do these compare or contrast? Explain your reasoning.**

Monday	Tuesday	Wednesday	Thursday	Friday
Calendar (TG p. 64) How would you describe this month's Calendar Pieces so far? **Computations and Connections** (TG p. 66) I have 3 friends. Each friend has 3 cookies. Can you fill the pockets with counters to match my story? **Clock** (TG p. 68) Where will the short hand be at today's time? Will it be right on the 11, midway, or far on its way to 12?	**Counting Tape and Hundred Chart** (TG p. 69) What day of school was it 7 school days ago? 17 days ago? 27 days ago? Describe the pattern. **Depositor** (TG p. 70) How do you write today's number in standard notation, expanded form and in words? **Coin Counter** (TG p. 71) What is today's total in the Coin Counter? What are three ways to represent today's amount in coins?	**Computations and Connections** (TG p. 66) I went to 5 booths at the fair yesterday. I won 3 trinkets at each booth. Can you fill the pockets with counters to match my story? **Clock** (TG p. 68) Draw what a clock looks like at 11:38. Where will the long minute hand be? Will it be closest to the 8, the 9 or the 10? Why?	**Counting Tape and Hundred Chart** (TG p. 69) How many 2s are in 78? How many 5s? How many 10s? **Depositor** (TG p. 70) What is the value of the digit in the hundreds place? How many days until we reach the next thousand? **Coin Counter** (TG p. 71) How much more money do we need to collect in the Coin Counter to get to one dollar?	**Calendar** (TG p. 64) Are the two trapezoids congruent? How could we find out? **Computations and Connections** (TG p. 66) Place 3 buttons in each of 4 pockets. How many pockets have buttons in them? How many buttons are in each? Can you tell a story that matches this picture?

TG refers to the Teacher's Guide.

© Houghton Mifflin Harcourt Publishing Company

December Week 2

Vocabulary This Month

Trapezoid, reflection, congruent, less than and greater than symbols (< and >), quarter till the hour

Update Questions

Be sure to ask: **What number? Is the number odd or even? What multiple? What amount? How many since? How long ago? What date? What shape? What color? What time?**

Elements for Number of Days in School

- Counting Tape and Hundred Chart (TG p. 69 Daily Routine)
- Depositor (TG p. 70 Daily Routine)
- Coin Counter (TG p. 71 Daily Routine)

Elements for Calendar Date

- Calendar (TG p. 64 Daily Routine)
- Computations and Connections (TG p. 66 Daily Routine)
- Clock (TG p. 68 Daily Routine)

Extras This Month

- Ending the Year (TG p. 64)

Discussion Questions

Follow up with these questions: **How do you know? How did you get your answer? How do these compare or contrast? Explain your reasoning.**

Monday	Tuesday	Wednesday	Thursday	Friday
Calendar (TG p. 64) Which pieces have blue stars? Describe that number pattern. **Computations and Connections** (TG p. 67) Can you fill the pockets to match the statement "6 groups of 2"? Describe it. **Clock** (TG p. 68) Read the time on the Clock. How many minutes is it after the hour? Before the next hour?	**Counting Tape and Hundred Chart** (TG p. 69) How many days has it been since Day 53? Since Day 28? **Depositor** (TG p. 70) What is your estimate of the amount of money in the Depositor on the last day of school before the holiday? How did you get to this amount?	**Computations and Connections** (TG p. 67) Draw a picture that shows how 6 packs of 3 pieces of gum (6 groups of 3) means the same as 6 × 3. **Coin Counter** (TG p. 71) What 2 Shopper Card items can we afford with today's coins? How can you estimate the total cost of the 2 items you chose?	**Counting Tape and Hundred Chart** (TG p. 69) What school days came between Day 64 and Day 73? **Depositor** (TG p. 70) Is there enough money in the Depositor to buy season tickets to the football games if they cost $5,000? How much more do we need? **Coin Counter** (TG p. 71) How could you make today's total with just dimes and pennies? What is another way to make today's total?	**Calendar** (TG p. 64) Will the blue stars always fall on the same shape? Why does that happen? **Computations and Connections** (TG p. 66) How would you explain what 3 × 4 means? **Clock** (TG p. 68) When someone says, "It is a quarter till 12," what time is it on the clock?

TG refers to the Teacher's Guide.

© Houghton Mifflin Harcourt Publishing Company

December Week 3

Vocabulary This Month

Trapezoid, reflection, congruent, less than and greater than symbols (< and >), quarter till the hour

Update Questions

Be sure to ask: **What number? Is the number odd or even? What multiple? What amount? How many since? How long ago? What date? What shape? What color? What time?**

Elements for Number of Days in School

- Counting Tape and Hundred Chart (TG p. 69 Daily Routine)
- Depositor (TG p. 70 Daily Routine)
- Coin Counter (TG p. 71 Daily Routine)

Elements for Calendar Date

- Calendar (TG p. 64 Daily Routine)
- Computations and Connections (TG p. 66 Daily Routine)
- Clock (TG p. 68 Daily Routine)

Extras This Month

- Ending the Year (TG p. 64)

Discussion Questions

Follow up with these questions: **How do you know? How did you get your answer? How do these compare or contrast? Explain your reasoning.**

Monday	Tuesday	Wednesday	Thursday	Friday
Calendar (TG p. 65) What term do you use to describe a shape that looks like it has been turned upside down? Can we use the same word to describe a shaped that has been flipped left to right? **Computations and Connections** (TG p. 67) What does the expression 3 + 3 + 3 look like with pockets and counters? What multiplication fact is equal to this addition expression?	**Counting Tape and Hundred Chart** (TG p. 69) How do you read the statement 73 < 100? How about 73 > 50? Describe other comparisons between two or more numbers. **Depositor** (TG p. 70) About how much money will we have when we add $73 to $2,628? How did you get your estimate?	**Coin Counter** (TG p. 71) Choose any two Shopper Cards to buy with today's total. Do you have enough to buy them? If yes, determine the change. If no, how much more do you need? **Clock** (TG p. 68) If a digital clock says 11:47, how many minutes past the hour is it?	**Counting Tape and Hundred Chart** (TG p. 69) How do you round 68 to the nearest ten? **Depositor** (TG p. 70) How much money will we add today? What is today's total? What strategy did you use? **Coin Counter** (TG p. 71) If you buy tape for 44¢ and a pencil for 17¢, what is the total cost? How did you get your answer?	**Calendar** (TG p. 65) How many of the trapezoids will it take to make a hexagon? What fraction name can we give to each trapezoid if the hexagon is the whole? **Computations and Connections** (TG p. 67) Who can tell a multiplication story that matches 4 × 5? Who can tell a different story? **Clock** (TG p. 68) What could the time be when the hour hand and the minute hand are almost touching the 12?

TG refers to the Teacher's Guide.

© Houghton Mifflin Harcourt Publishing Company

December Week 4

Vocabulary This Month

Trapezoid, reflection, congruent, less than and greater than symbols (< and >), quarter till the hour

Update Questions

***Be sure to ask:* What number? Is the number odd or even? What multiple? What amount? How many since? How long ago? What date? What shape? What color? What time?**

Elements for Number of Days in School

- Counting Tape and Hundred Chart (TG p. 69 Daily Routine)
- Depositor (TG p. 70 Daily Routine)
- Coin Counter (TG p. 71 Daily Routine)

Elements for Calendar Date

- Calendar (TG p. 64 Daily Routine)
- Computations and Connections (TG p. 66 Daily Routine)
- Clock (TG p. 68 Daily Routine)

Extras This Month

- Ending the Year (TG p. 64)

Discussion Questions

***Follow up with these questions:* How do you know? How did you get your answer? How do these compare or contrast? Explain your reasoning.**

Monday	Tuesday	Wednesday	Thursday	Friday
Calendar (TG p. 65) Describe the number pattern of the trapezoid Calendar Pieces that are the top half of the hexagon. Bottom half? What is the difference between these Calendar Pieces? **Computations and Connections** (TG p. 66) What story problem can you tell that could be solved by multiplying? **Clock** (TG p. 68) If the time were 3 minutes from the time shown, where would the long minute hand be?	**Counting Tape and Hundred Chart** (TG p. 70) What day of school will it be in 20 more school days? In 18 more days? What strategies did you use to solve these problems? **Depositor** (TG p. 70) How many thousands are in today's number? Hundreds? How would you tell me the number using only hundreds, tens, and ones?	**Calendar** (TG p. 64) A hexagon can be made by combining two trapezoids. Can you think of another shape that can be made by combining two congruent shapes? **Coin Counter** (TG p. 71) You purchase gum for 16¢ and a pencil for 17¢. What strategy would you use to make your purchase? How much change would you receive? Explain.	**Counting Tape and Hundred Chart** (TG p. 70) Which numbers could be rounded to 60 if you were rounding to the nearest 10? **Depositor** (TG p. 70) How much money would remain if we bought gifts that cost $575? Explain your thinking. **Coin Counter** (TG p. 71) Do you have enough money to buy the two most expensive Shopper Card items? How did you determine your answer?	**Calendar** (TG p. 65) Do the hexagons look like they are rotated? Could they be? Explain. **Computations and Connections** (TG p. 66) In what situations would you multiply to solve a problem? **Clock** (TG p. 68) If we started at 11:30 and moved the Clock one minute per the day's date in December, what time would it be on December 31st?

TG refers to the Teacher's Guide.

© Houghton Mifflin Harcourt Publishing Company

Big Math Ideas This Month

Examine three-dimensional shapes; explore multiples of 3; develop strategies for multiplication and division facts; understand area and perimeter; express numbers in various notations; collect, organize, and analyze data in a bar graph

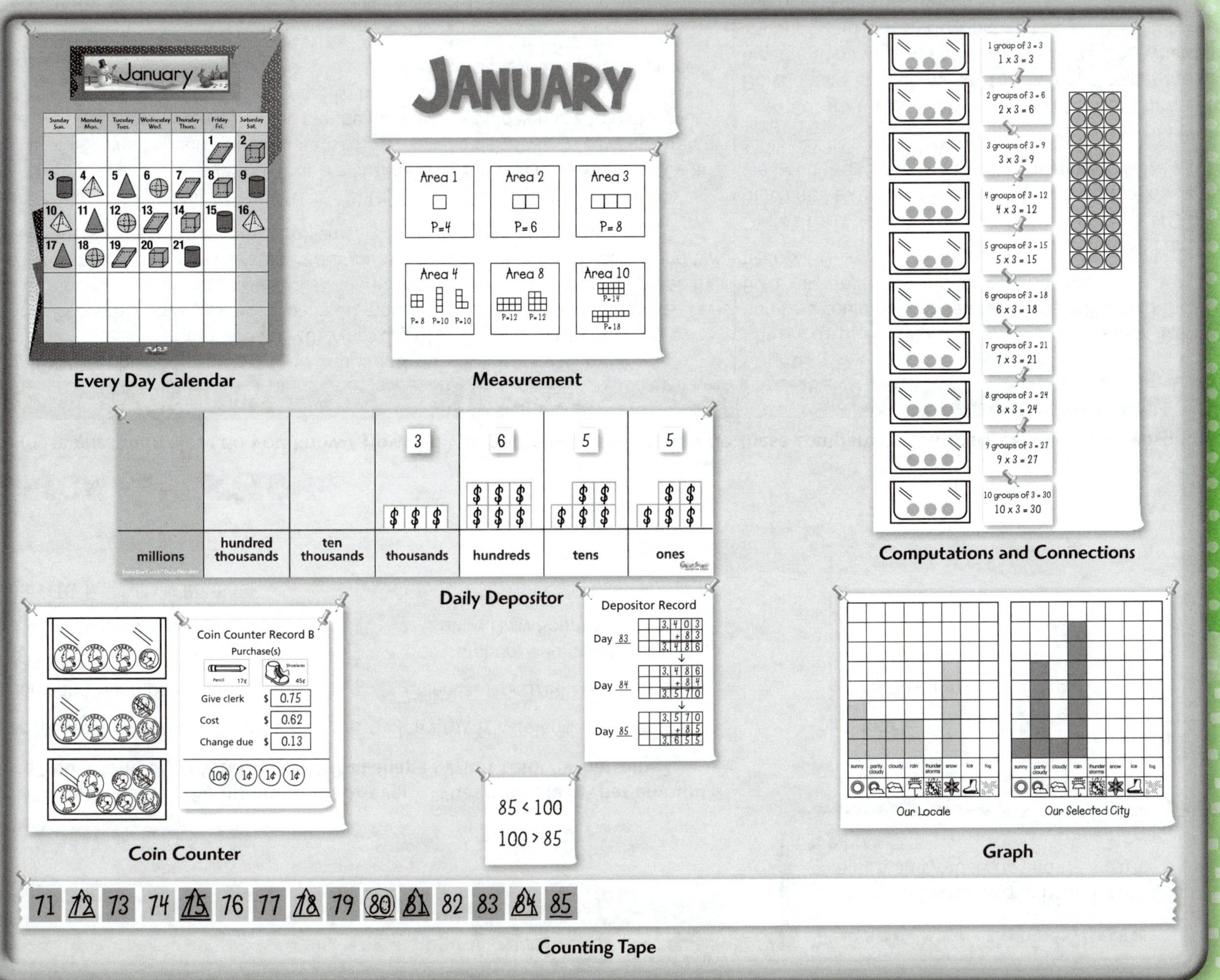

© Houghton Mifflin Harcourt Publishing Company

MONTHLY RESOURCES

INTERVENTION

- **Area and Perimeter: Small Group:** Because many times perimeter and area are taught together, students may have trouble distinguishing between the two. Define perimeter as a linear measurement that covers the distance around a figure, where area is a measure of how much surface is covered by a figure. Before students explore these two concepts on graph paper, use color tiles and lengths of string or yarn to explore the perimeter and area of different figures that they create. After students freely explore these concepts, have them construct figures with a given perimeter or area and compare the relationship. For the Measurement this month, the figures cannot be congruent and thus the concepts of slides, flips and turns must also be investigated.

- **Sums in a Sequence: Small Group:** The strategy of multiplying the number of odd numbers in a sequence by the middle number in that sequence can be conceptually difficult for students without a visual to accompany it. Using cubes or blocks, make three piles—one with 1 block, another with 2 blocks stacked, and a third with 3 blocks stacked. Ask students to try to find a way to make the stacks the same by moving 1 block. Explain that this is like adding a three-number in sequence—1 + 2 + 3. If you take 1 off the third stack and put it on the first stack, it will have 2, as will the second and third stacks. Taking 1 off the greatest stack and adding it onto the smallest stack makes them all the same as the middle number. Try this with a few other sums of three numbers in a sequence and ask students to compose a theory about three numbers in a sequence added together. Something like this might be the outcome of the discussion: *The sum of three numbers in order is equal to three times the middle number*. This method applies to the sum of any odd set of numbers in sequence.

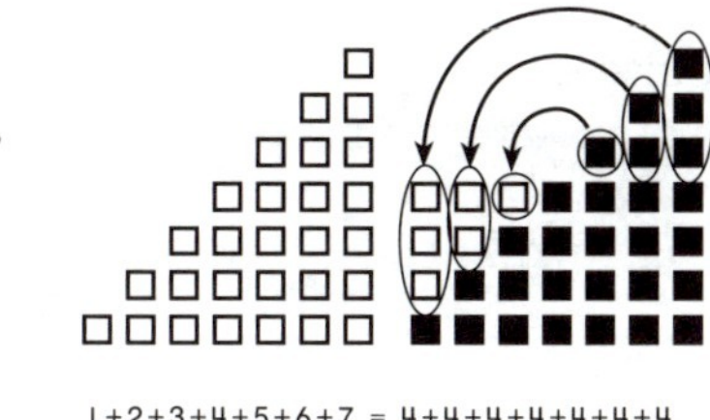

MORE HELPFUL HINTS

- One Hundredth Day Celebration: If your 100th day of school comes in January, see February's elements for suggestions of activities to be used for this day.

- Calendar: Have students bring in real life examples of three-dimensional solids to use to explore the attributes of the solids on the Calendar Pieces.

- Counting Tape and Computations and Connections: Because the Counting Tape and Computations and Connections explore the multiples of 3, create picture posters of the "times 3" facts. Students can use ideas from a discussion of things that come in 3s at the beginning of Computations and Connections. It is important for students to pause and record a number sentence each time they add a new group of three to their charts.

Picture Poster for 3
x = "groups of"

(1 group of utensils)	1 x 3 = 3
(2 groups of utensils)	2 x 3 = 6
(3 groups of utensils)	3 x 3 = 9

Picture Poster for 3
x = "groups of"

(tricycles)	1 x 3 = 3
(tricycles)	2 x 3 = 6

ASSESSMENTS

January Assessment: See pages 89–92.

Winter Test: See pages 61–64.

Multiplication Facts Progress Record: See page 112.

Assessment Checklist: See pages 109–110.

© Houghton Mifflin Harcourt Publishing Company

January Week 1

Vocabulary This Month

Rectangular prism, cube, cylinder, pyramid, cone, sphere, edge, multiple, area, perimeter

Update Questions

Be sure to ask: **What number? Is the number odd or even? What multiple? What amount? How many since? How long ago? What date? What shape? What coins? What time?**

Elements for Number of Days in School

- Counting Tape and Hundred Chart (TG p. 80 Daily Routine)
- Depositor (TG p. 82 Daily Routine)
- Coin Counter (TG p. 83 Daily Routine)

Elements for Calendar Date

- Calendar (TG p. 74 Daily Routine)
- Computations and Connections (TG p. 77 Daily Routine)
- Measurement (TG p. 79 Daily Routine)

Extras This Month

- Graph (TG p. 85 Daily Routine)

Discussion Questions

Follow up with these questions: **How do you know? How did you get your answer? How do these compare or contrast? Explain your reasoning.**

Monday	Tuesday	Wednesday	Thursday	Friday
Calendar (TG p. 74) How would you describe the Calendar Pieces for this month? **Computations and Connections** (TG p. 77) Can you use the list of threes to tell a story about today's amount? Write a number sentence to match. **Measurement** (TG p. 78) How would you describe what the word *area* means? How would you describe *perimeter*?	**Counting Tape and Hundred Chart** (TG p. 80) What are the first four multiples of 3 on the Counting Tape? How do you know? **Depositor** (TG p. 82) What is the difference between your estimate of today's amount and today's actual amount? **Coin Counter** (TG p. 84) What coins would you choose to make today's amount?	**Graph** (TG p. 85) Look at October's weather graph. Make predictions about the number of sunny days, rainy days and snowy days January will have compared to October. Compare the two weather graphs at the end of the month. **Measurement** (TG p. 78) How many square units will you use to make today's figure? What is the area? What is its perimeter?	**Counting Tape and Hundred Chart** (TG p. 80) How can you decide whether today's number is a multiple of 3? Is it? **Depositor** (TG p. 82) What is today's total written in expanded notation? In words? **Coin Counter** (TG p. 84) Using the least number of coins, how many coins will you need to make today's total? What is another way to make today's total?	**Calendar** (TG p. 75) Name the solid shapes that have appeared on the Calendar so far. Describe their faces and/or bases. **Computations and Connections** (TG p. 77) How many pockets have counters in them? How many counters are in each? Can you tell a story that matches this picture? **Measurement** (TG p. 78) Why is area measured in square units?

TG refers to the Teacher's Guide.

© Houghton Mifflin Harcourt Publishing Company

January Week 2

Vocabulary This Month

Rectangular prism, cube, cylinder, pyramid, cone, sphere, edge, multiple, area, perimeter

Update Questions

Be sure to ask: **What number? Is the number odd or even? What multiple? What amount? How many since? How long ago? What date? What shape? What coins? What time?**

Elements for Number of Days in School

- Counting Tape and Hundred Chart (TG p. 80 Daily Routine)
- Depositor (TG p. 82 Daily Routine)
- Coin Counter (TG p. 83 Daily Routine)

Elements for Calendar Date

- Calendar (TG p. 74 Daily Routine)
- Computations and Connections (TG p. 77 Daily Routine)
- Measurement (TG p. 79 Daily Routine)

Extras This Month

- Graph (TG p. 85 Daily Routine)

Discussion Questions

Follow up with these questions: **How do you know? How did you get your answer? How do these compare or contrast? Explain your reasoning.**

Monday	Tuesday	Wednesday	Thursday	Friday
Calendar (TG pp. 74–75) What solid is on today's Calendar Piece? How many faces and/or bases does it have? What are the shapes of the faces and/or bases? **Computations and Connections** (TG p. 77) How many groups of three are there so far? Describe today's array. **Measurement** (TG p. 79) How many square units will you use to make today's figure? What is your figure's perimeter?	**Counting Tape and Hundred Chart** (TG p. 80) What is today's number rounded to the nearest ten? What are some other numbers that can be rounded to that same ten? **Depositor** (TG p. 82) What is today's amount in standard form? What is today's number using only hundreds, tens and ones? **Coin Counter** (TG p. 84) What two items can we purchase with today's amount?	**Graph** (TG p. 85) How many sunny days have been forecast for us this month compared to our selected city? How do cloudy days compare? Rainy? **Measurement** (TG p. 79) How many square units are in today's figure? If you create another figure with the same area, how can you be sure that the figures are not congruent?	**Counting Tape and Hundred Chart** (TG p. 80) How many groups of 3 are in today's number? Can we check by counting 10 threes at a time, and then count what is left by threes? **Depositor** (TG p. 82) If a family has saved $4,095 and spends $500 on a camping trip, about how much money will they have left? **Coin Counter** (TG p. 83) What is the value of 3 quarters, 1 nickel, and 2 pennies?	**Calendar** (TG pp. 74–75) Which solid shapes have similar attributes? Describe them. **Computations and Connections** (TG p. 77) What is our total number of counters? How many rows of three are in our array? Write a number sentence to match. **Measurement** (TG p. 79) Can you find any shapes you made this month that have the same perimeter, but have different areas?

TG refers to the Teacher's Guide.

© Houghton Mifflin Harcourt Publishing Company

January Week 3

Vocabulary This Month

Rectangular prism, cube, cylinder, pyramid, cone, sphere, edge, multiple, area, perimeter

Update Questions

Be sure to ask: **What number? Is the number odd or even? What multiple? What amount? How many since? How long ago? What date? What shape? What coins? What time?**

Elements for Number of Days in School

- Counting Tape and Hundred Chart (TG p. 80 Daily Routine)
- Depositor (TG p. 82 Daily Routine)
- Coin Counter (TG p. 83 Daily Routine)

Elements for Calendar Date

- Calendar (TG p. 74 Daily Routine)
- Computations and Connections (TG p. 77 Daily Routine)
- Measurement (TG p. 79 Daily Routine)

Extras This Month

- Graph (TG p. 85 Daily Routine)

Discussion Questions

Follow up with these questions: **How do you know? How did you get your answer? How do these compare or contrast? Explain your reasoning.**

Monday	Tuesday	Wednesday	Thursday	Friday
Calendar (TG pp. 74–75) What will be the date on the last cube? The last rectangular prism? The last cylinder? The last pyramid? The last cone? The last sphere? **Computations and Connections** (TG p. 77) Write an addition sentence to match the amount in 5 pockets. Tell a story to match. **Measurement** (TG p. 80) Arrange the squares in today's figure to show the longest perimeter and the shortest perimeter.	**Counting Tape and Hundred Chart** (TG p. 80) How many days has it been since Day 50? How many days until Day 100? Which comparison has the biggest difference? **Depositor** (TG p. 82) Use a "sums in sequence" strategy to add 18 + 19 + 20 + 21 + 22. **Coin Counter** (TG p. 84) What two items can we purchase with today's amount?	**Graph** (TG p. 85) How many days this month would rain need to be forecast here at home for the rainy days to equal the rainy days forecast in our selected city? **Computations and Connections** (TG p. 77) How could you write an addition sentence to match 7 rows in our array? Tell a story to match.	**Counting Tape and Hundred Chart** (TG p. 80) How do we use the less than and greater than symbols to compare today's number to 100? **Depositor** (TG p. 82) What is today's amount written in words? In expanded form? **Coin Counter** (TG p. 84) If you have 3 quarters and buy a pen for 59¢, what will your change be? Can you buy another item from our Shopper Cards?	**Calendar** (TG pp. 74–75) If the pyramid had a pentagon for a base, how many triangular faces would it have? Why? **Computations and Connections** (TG p. 77) Use the pockets and counters to show 4 × 3. Now show 3 × 4. Compare and contrast the two pictures. **Measurement** (TG p. 80) Do figures with the same area always have the same perimeter? How do you know?

TG refers to the Teacher's Guide.

© Houghton Mifflin Harcourt Publishing Company

January Week 4

Vocabulary This Month

Rectangular prism, cube, cylinder, pyramid, cone, sphere, edge, multiple, area, perimeter

Update Questions

Be sure to ask: **What number? Is the number odd or even? What multiple? What amount? How many since? How long ago? What date? What shape? What coins? What time?**

Elements for Number of Days in School

- Counting Tape and Hundred Chart (TG p. 80 Daily Routine)
- Depositor (TG p. 82 Daily Routine)
- Coin Counter (TG p. 83 Daily Routine)

Elements for Calendar Date

- Calendar (TG p. 74 Daily Routine)
- Computations and Connections (TG p. 77 Daily Routine)
- Measurement (TG p. 79 Daily Routine)

Extras This Month

- Graph (TG p. 85 Daily Routine)

Discussion Questions

Follow up with these questions: **How do you know? How did you get your answer? How do these compare or contrast? Explain your reasoning.**

Monday	Tuesday	Wednesday	Thursday	Friday
Calendar (TG p. 74) Why are the rectangular prism and the cube the same color on the Calendar Pieces? **Computations and Connections** (TG p. 76) Describe how you find the answer to 6 × 3. 7 × 3? 8 × 3? 9 × 3? **Measurement** (TG p. 78) Can you use today's squares to make figures with two different perimeters? Can you make another?	**Counting Tape and Hundred Chart** (TG p. 80) Where does the 7th triangle appear? The 15th triangle? **Depositor** (TG p. 83) Play *Beat the Calculator*. Half the class uses mental math and half the class uses calculators to find the sum of three numbers in a sequence. Add 2 + 3 + 4. Add 5 + 6 + 7. Add 10 + 11 + 12. Add 20 + 21 + 22. Add 29 + 30 + 31.	**Graph** (TG p. 85) Using both Graphs, what is the total number of sunny days? The difference between sunny and rainy or snowy days? Based on the actual weather, have the forecasts been fairly accurate? **Measurement** (TG p. 80) What have you noticed during the month about the shapes that have the longest perimeter each day?	**Counting Tape and Hundred Chart** (TG p. 80) Can you find a number that will divide into groups of 3 and into groups of 5 with no leftovers? Describe these numbers. **Depositor** (TG p. 82) Have you changed your estimate for how much money you think we will collect by the end of the year? Explain. **Coin Counter** (TG p. 84) Which two items could you buy and receive the most change from the amount in the Coin Counter?	**Calendar** (TG p. 75) Do you see the two patterns? Describe them. How many of these shapes slide? Roll? Stack? **Computations and Connections** (TG p. 76) What are the similarities between this month's rule and the triangles on the Counting Tape? Explain. **Measurement** (TG p. 78) Draw two figures, each with an area of ten square units, but with perimeters that are not the same.

TG refers to the Teacher's Guide.

© Houghton Mifflin Harcourt Publishing Company

Big Math Ideas This Month

Examine fractions of a circle; explore multiples of 4; convert capacity between ounces, cups, pints, and quarts; add and subtract mentally; explore relationship between sample size and theoretical probability

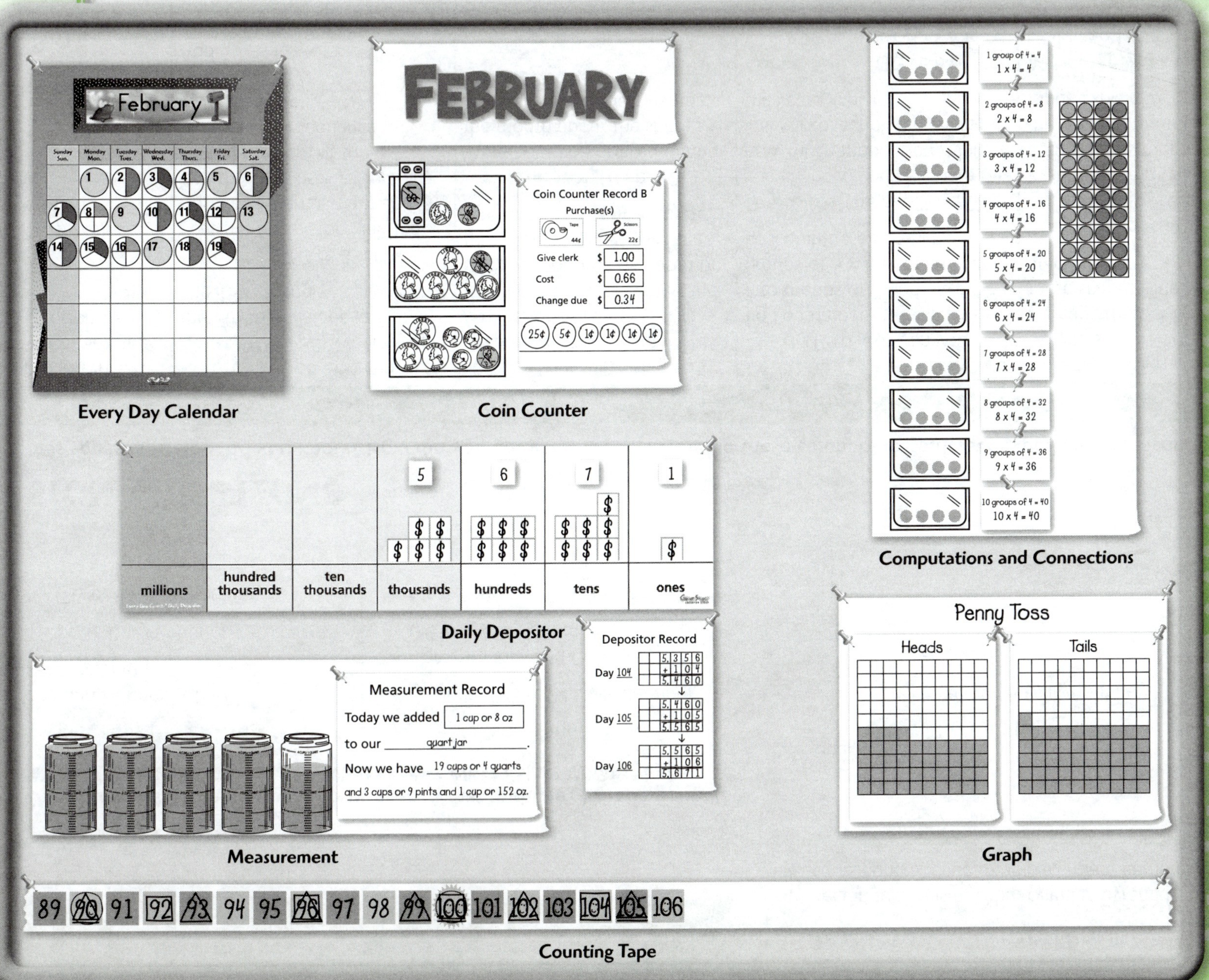

© Houghton Mifflin Harcourt Publishing Company

Monthly Resources

Intervention

- **Multiples of 4: Small Group:** Students may know the number word sequence for the multiples of 4, but may not know them past the number 20 (**4, 8, 12, 16, 20** …24…28…32, etc.) nor realize that they are counting by a quantity of 4. Explain multiples as numbers that can be grouped by the given number or separated into groups of the given number. Pass out bags of counters that represent an amount for different days that they have been in school. Let them explore whether their amount is a multiple of 4 by separating it into 4 groups or into groups of 4 with no leftovers. If their amount is a group of 4 with no leftovers, have them draw a square around that number on the Counting Tape. Having them manipulate the counters into the groups helps with the conceptual understanding of multiples instead of only seeing it as a group of counting numerals.
- **100th Day: Small Group:** Unlike primary grades where students may simply bring in a collection of 100 things, have the students bring or design 100 items into the multiples that have been discovered over the course of the school year: multiples of 2, 3, 4, 5 and 10. In small groups, divide these items into the different groups and discuss why there may or may not be remaining items after they have been separated. Try this with smaller amounts as well.
- **Multiples of 4 as Groups of 2: Small Group:** Use counters and Circular Array Paper (TR14) to prove that numbers that can be broken into groups of 4 can also be broken into groups of 2. Many students are comfortable with skip counting by 2s and grouping by 2s, so making the connection that groups of 2 can be doubled to make groups of 4 may help in solving problems where the multiple of 4 is not known.

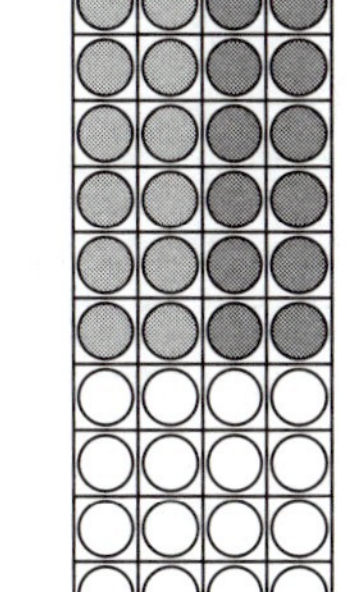

More Helpful Hints

- Calendar: Use Calendar Pieces (TR 26) for students to explore the fractional relationships on this month's Calendar Pieces. Allow them to color them like the Calendar Pieces on the Calendar, then cut them out and compare to the real Calendar as well as to the "whole" from which each fraction is a part.
- Counting Tape: If you have students make a vertical list of the multiples of 4 and say the pattern in the ones place, they may find the auditory pattern helpful in learning to count by 4s with ease. Also, repeat the whole number sequence to develop fluency.
- Measurement: If available, using real containers that can be filled with blue colored water will allow students to conceptualize the capacity of the container instead of just coloring in the recording sheet.

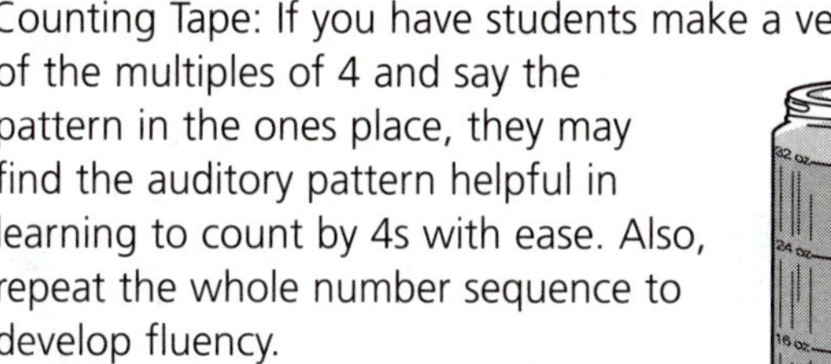

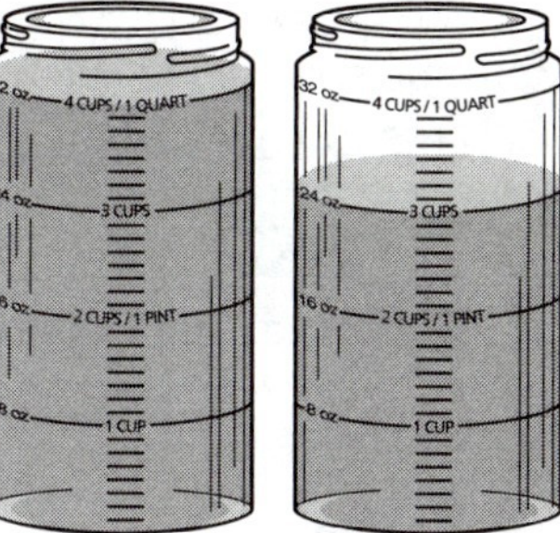

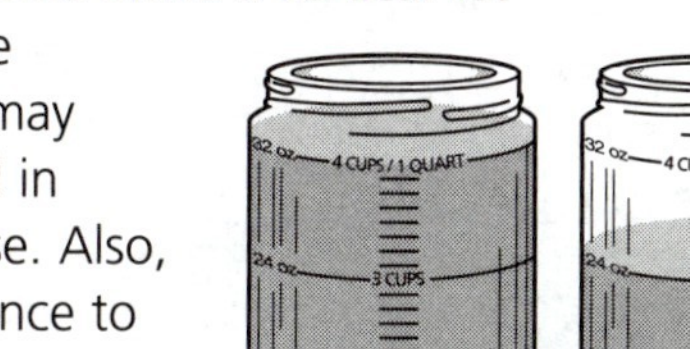

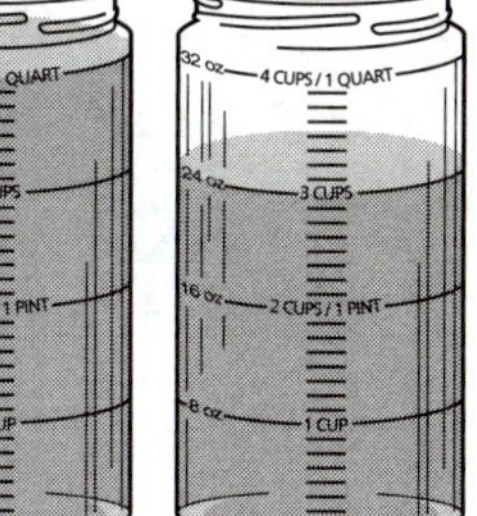

Measurement Record

Today we added  1 cup or 8 oz

to our quart jar.

Now we have 7 cups or 1 quart

and 3 cups, or 3 pints and 1 cup, or 56 oz.

Assessments

February Assessment: See pages 93–96.

Multiplication Facts Progress Record: See page 112.

Assessment Checklist: See pages 109–110.

© Houghton Mifflin Harcourt Publishing Company

February Week 1

Vocabulary This Month

Fractional piece, numerator, denominator, half, third, fourth, ounce, cup, pint, quart, capacity, sample size, probability experiment

Update Questions

Be sure to ask: **How many? What number? What date? Is the number odd or even? What multiple? What amount? What coins? What fraction?**

Elements for Number of Days in School

- Counting Tape and Hundred Chart (TG p. 94 Daily Routine)
- Daily Depositor (TG p. 95 Daily Routine)
- Coin Counter (TG p. 97 Daily Routine)

Elements for Calendar Date

- Calendar (TG p. 88 Daily Routine)
- Computations and Connections (TG p. 90 Daily Routine)

Extras This Month

- One Hundredth Day Celebration (TG p. 88)
- Graph (TG p. 98 Daily Routine)
- Measurement (TG p. 92 Daily Routine)

Discussion Questions

Follow up with these questions: **How do you know? How did you get your answer? How do these compare or contrast? Explain your reasoning.**

Monday	Tuesday	Wednesday	Thursday	Friday
Calendar (TG p. 89) How would you describe the Calendar Pieces for this month so far? **Computations and Connections** (TG p. 90) Can you use the list of 4s to tell a story about today's amount? Write a number sentence to match. **Measurement** (TG p. 92) This month liquid will be measured with ounces, cups, pints and quarts. List them in order from smallest to largest unit.	**Counting Tape and Hundred Chart** (TG p. 94) What are the first four multiples of 4 on the Counting Tape? How do you know? **Depositor** (TG p. 95) How many hundred dollar bills would you get in exchange for today's total? **Coin Counter** (TG p. 97) How can we show today's amount with the least amount of coins? Give two other combinations.	**Graph** (TG p. 98) If a student tosses the penny 5 times each day we are at school, how many days until we reach our sample size of 100 tosses? **One Hundredth Day Activity: Coin Counter** (TG p. 97) Challenge students to find as many different combinations of coins that they can to equal $1.	**Counting Tape and Hundred Chart** (TG p. 95) How many groups of 4 are in today's number? Are there any extras? On what day will the next multiple of 4 appear? **Depositor** (TG p. 96) Which thousand is today's total closest to? What is the difference between the two numbers? **Coin Counter** (TG p. 97) What is the value of 2 quarters, 3 dimes, 3 nickels, and 3 pennies?	**Calendar** (TG p. 89) How many equal parts are shown in this circle? How many of those equal parts are colored? **Computations and Connections** (TG p. 90) What is our total number of counters? How many rows of four are in our array? Write a number sentence to match. **Measurement** (TG p. 92) If we continue to add 1 cup each day, how many quart jars do you think we will fill by the end of the month?

TG refers to the Teacher's Guide.

© Houghton Mifflin Harcourt Publishing Company

February Week 2

Vocabulary This Month

Fractional piece, numerator, denominator, half, third, fourth, ounce, cup, pint, quart, capacity, sample size, probability experiment

Update Questions

Be sure to ask: **How many? What number? What date? Is the number odd or even? What multiple? What amount? What coins? What fraction?**

Elements for Number of Days in School

- Counting Tape and Hundred Chart (TG p. 94 Daily Routine)
- Daily Depositor (TG p. 95 Daily Routine)
- Coin Counter (TG p. 97 Daily Routine)

Elements for Calendar Date

- Calendar (TG p. 88 Daily Routine)
- Computations and Connections (TG p. 90 Daily Routine)

Extras This Month

- One Hundredth Day Celebration (TG p. 88)
- Graph (TG p. 98 Daily Routine)
- Measurement (TG p. 92 Daily Routine)

Discussion Questions

Follow up with these questions: **How do you know? How did you get your answer? How do these compare or contrast? Explain your reasoning.**

Monday	Tuesday	Wednesday	Thursday	Friday
Calendar (TG p. 89) What numbers are on the whole pieces? What will the next whole piece be? How do you know? **Computations and Connections** (TG p. 90) How many groups of four are there so far? Describe today's array. **Measurement** (TG p. 91) How many cups are in 4 quarts? How did you figure that out?	**Counting Tape and Hundred Chart** (TG p. 95) What number will today's number round to if we are rounding to the nearest 10? To the nearest 100? **Depositor** (TG p. 96) What is today's total? What strategy did you use to add the day's amount? **Coin Counter** (TG p. 98) Refer to our list of combinations of coins to equal $1. How many solutions use 3 quarters?	**Graph** (TG p. 98) If you get heads 39 times after 100 tosses, what fraction of the total is that? **One Hundredth Day Activity: Depositor** (TG p. 96) Explore different strategies to find out the amount in the Depositor on the 100th day of school. Have students pair the numbers 1–100 with lowest number paired with highest number until they have 50 pairs. Can you use this to find the amount on the 100th day?	**Counting Tape and Hundred Chart** (TG p. 93) How many groups of 4 are in 20? In 32? In 48? Do any of these numbers have groups of 3? Which ones? **Depositor** (TG p. 97) How could we round today's amount to the nearest ten dollars? **Coin Counter** (TG p. 97) What coins would you use to make 90 cents if you had no dimes?	**Calendar** (TG p. 32) Is the colored portion of today's Calendar Piece greater or less than the colored portion on the last Calendar Piece? Name the two fractions. **Computations and Connections** (TG p. 90) How many groups of 2 are in each row of the array? How can knowing your "times 2" facts help you know your "times 4" facts? **Measurement** (TG p. 91) How many ounces are in 2 cups? In 2 pints?

TG refers to the Teacher's Guide.

© Houghton Mifflin Harcourt Publishing Company

February Week 3

Vocabulary This Month

Fractional piece, numerator, denominator, half, third, fourth, ounce, cup, pint, quart, capacity, sample size, probability experiment

Update Questions

Be sure to ask: **How many? What number? What date? Is the number odd or even? What multiple? What amount? What coins? What fraction?**

Elements for Number of Days in School

- Counting Tape and Hundred Chart (TG p. 94 Daily Routine)
- Daily Depositor (TG p. 95 Daily Routine)
- Coin Counter (TG p. 97 Daily Routine)

Elements for Calendar Date

- Calendar (TG p. 88 Daily Routine)
- Computations and Connections (TG p. 90 Daily Routine)

Extras This Month

- One Hundredth Day Celebration (TG p. 88)
- Graph (TG p. 98 Daily Routine)
- Measurement (TG p. 92 Daily Routine)

Discussion Questions

Follow up with these questions: **How do you know? How did you get your answer? How do these compare or contrast? Explain your reasoning.**

Monday	Tuesday	Wednesday	Thursday	Friday
Calendar (TG p. 89) What piece should go on the Calendar today? How do you know? What Calendar Piece will appear a week from now? **Computations and Connections** (TG p. 90) Write an addition sentence to match the amount in 5 pockets. Tell a story to match. **Measurement** (TG p. 91) 12 cups is the same as how many quarts? How did you get your answer?	**Counting Tape and Hundred Chart** (TG p. 94) How many school days have we had since Day 73? Day 65? **Depositor** (TG p. 97) In about how many days will we trade for our next thousand dollar bill? What day of school might that be? **Coin Counter** (TG p. 97) What two items can we purchase with today's amount?	**Graph** (TG p. 98) If you get tails 51 times after 100 tosses, what decimal is that? What percent is that? **One Hundredth Day Activity: Coin Counter** (TG p. 98) Revisit the coin combinations that can equal $1. How can you be sure that you have listed all the possibilities?	**Counting Tape and Hundred Chart** (TG p. 94) Which multiples of 2 have squares around them? Which multiples of 4 are even numbers? **Depositor** (TG p. 97) If we spent $2,000 on a new computer, about how much money would we have left? What would the exact amount be? **Coin Counter** (TG p. 97) How could we make today's amount with only dimes and pennies? With only nickels and pennies?	**Calendar** (TG p. 88) What fractional part is shown on the Calendar by all the multiples of 4? **Computations and Connections** (TG p. 90) How can knowing that $7 \times 2 = 14$ help you learn 7×4? **Measurement** (TG p. 93) How many cups do we have today? How many quarts is that? How many extra cups?

TG refers to the Teacher's Guide.

© Houghton Mifflin Harcourt Publishing Company

February Week 4

Vocabulary This Month

Fractional piece, numerator, denominator, half, third, fourth, ounce, cup, pint, quart, capacity, sample size, probability experiment

Update Questions

Be sure to ask: **How many? What number? What date? Is the number odd or even? What multiple? What amount? What coins? What fraction?**

Elements for Number of Days in School

- Counting Tape and Hundred Chart (TG p. 94 Daily Routine)
- Daily Depositor (TG p. 95 Daily Routine)
- Coin Counter (TG p. 97 Daily Routine)

Elements for Calendar Date

- Calendar (TG p. 88 Daily Routine)
- Computations and Connections (TG p. 90 Daily Routine)

Extras This Month

- One Hundredth Day Celebration (TG p. 88)
- Graph (TG p. 98 Daily Routine)
- Measurement (TG p. 92 Daily Routine)

Discussion Questions

Follow up with these questions: **How do you know? How did you get your answer? How do these compare or contrast? Explain your reasoning.**

Monday	Tuesday	Wednesday	Thursday	Friday
Calendar (TG p. 89) If we increase the number of equal parts, do the parts get larger or smaller in size? How does this affect the denominator of a fraction? **Computations and Connections** (TG p. 90) What are the similarities between this month's rule and the squares on the Counting Tape? Explain. **Measurement** (TG p. 92) How many cups are in a pint? A quart?	**Counting Tape and Hundred Chart** (TG p. 95) How many tens are in 100? How many twos? How many fives? Fours? Are there any leftovers in these amounts? **Depositor** (TG p. 96) What digit is in the hundreds place? The tens place? What is the value of each of these? **Coin Counter** (TG p. 97) A snack costs $1.52. How much more money do you need to buy it?	**Graph** (TG p. 98) What is the likelihood of getting heads or tails when you toss a penny? Explain how you know. **One Hundredth Day Activity: Graph** (TG p. 98) Have students work in pairs to toss a penny ten times. Combine all the results to compare to the Penny Toss Graph. Were the results similar? Should they be? Explain.	**Counting Tape and Hundred Chart** (TG p. 95) Which days have a triangle and a square around them? Explain why that happens. **Depositor** (TG p. 97) Have you changed your estimate for how much money you think we will collect by the end of the year? Explain. **Coin Counter** (TG p. 97) If you buy a snack for 87¢ with $1, how much change will you receive?	**Calendar** (TG p. 88) Why is $\frac{1}{4}$ smaller than $\frac{1}{3}$, even though 4 is greater than 3? **Computations and Connections** (TG p. 90) What are the similarities between the 2 groups of 2 in this month's array and the two colored self-stick notes on the Counting Tape? **Measurement** (TG p. 93) How many cups have been collected this month? How many quarts?

TG refers to the Teacher's Guide.

© Houghton Mifflin Harcourt Publishing Company

Big Math Ideas This Month

Describe a growing pattern, explore multiples of 5, explore division as sharing equally among groups, convert weight between ounces and pounds, calculate elapsed time, round to the nearest hundred ten, solve problems with coins

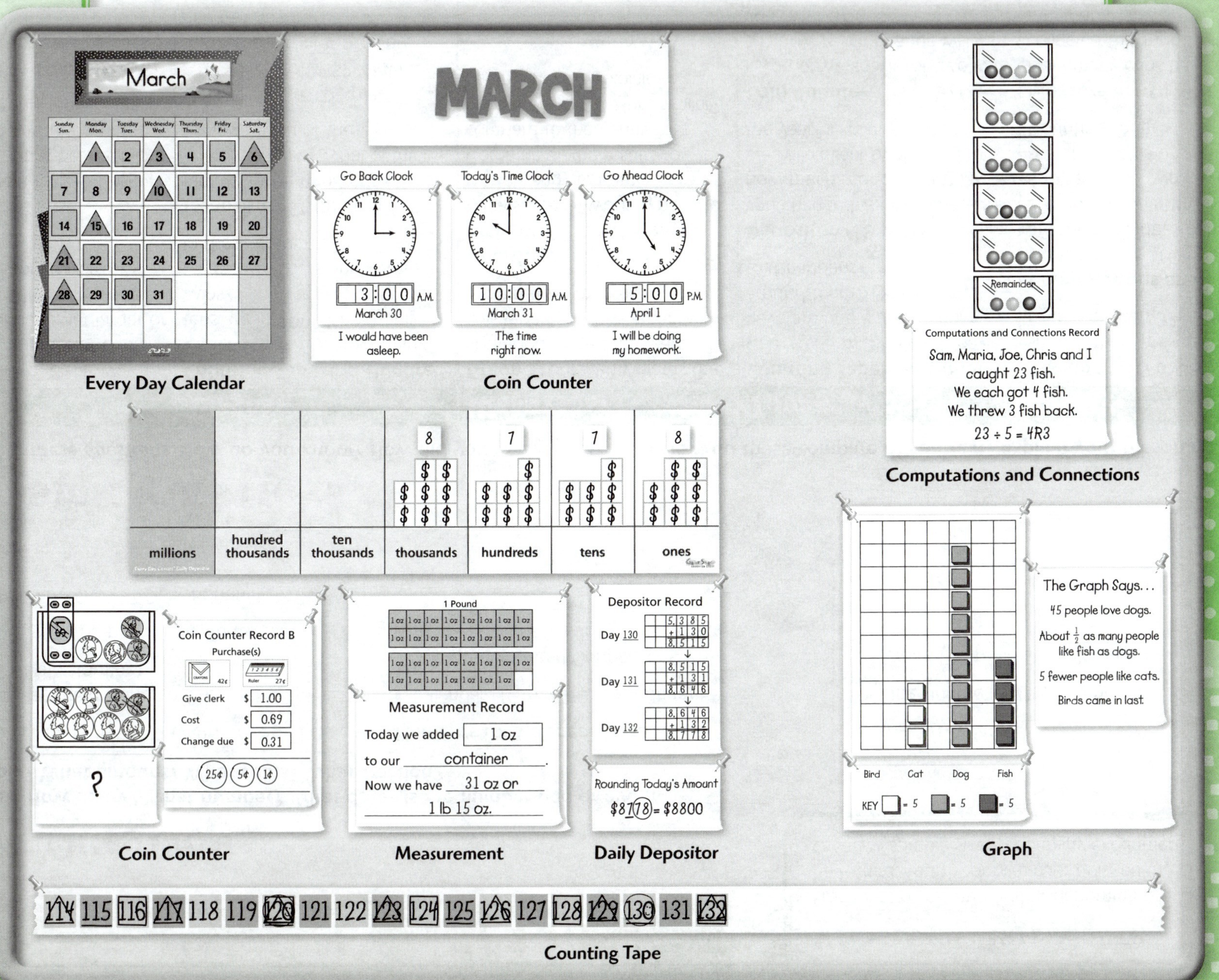

© Houghton Mifflin Harcourt Publishing Company

Monthly Resources

Intervention

- **Division: Small Group:** This may be the first experience with division for some students. Because the formation of equal groups is critical in the understanding of division, opportunities for the students to physically represent division stories is essential. Allow students to use counters to share a given number of counters equally among a given number of groups. Students should experience problems with and without remainders. Use everyday language in telling division stories and begin writing the corresponding number sentence when appropriate. In turn, have students tell stories and group counters that correspond to given number sentences.

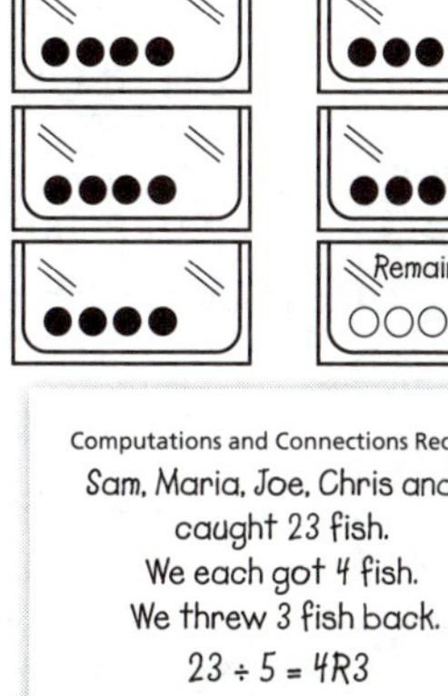

- **Elapsed Time: Small Group:** This month's *Go Back Clock* and *Go Ahead Clock* can be especially confusing for students when the given time must go back or ahead across 12:00 and change the hour from A.M. to P.M. and vice versa. Allow students to use clocks with gears to change the time hour by hour so they can count each hour as they change the time. Discuss different strategies for adding or subtracting using common benchmarks on the clock such as 12:00, 3:00, 6:00 and 9:00. A smaller copy of Clock (TR12) for students to manipulate at their desks may also prove useful.

- **Rounding to the Nearest Hundred: Small Group:** Creating a number line from 0 to 1,000 (and later from 0 to 10,000) can help students see the placement of larger numbers and give a visual for rounding numbers to the hundreds and thousands. Create cards with given numbers and have students discuss placement on the number line and to which hundred or thousand each is closest. Discuss numerical clues that may help students in deciding to which number the given number can be rounded, but always have students prove their answers by giving the difference (or distance) between the two numbers.

More Helpful Hints

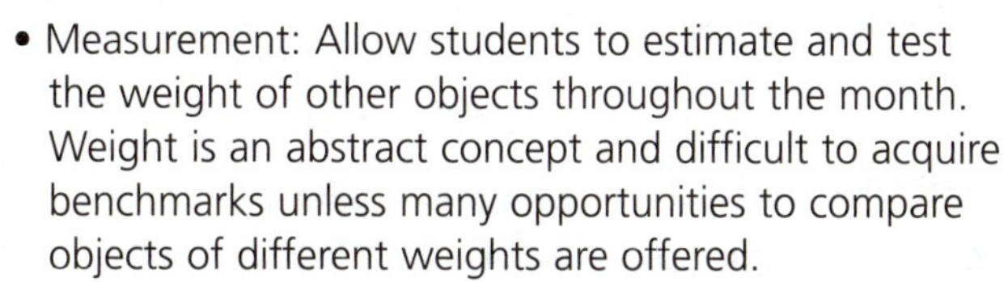

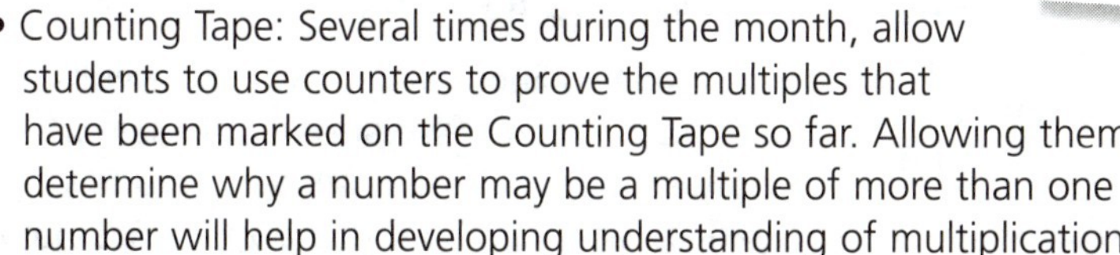

- Measurement: Allow students to estimate and test the weight of other objects throughout the month. Weight is an abstract concept and difficult to acquire benchmarks unless many opportunities to compare objects of different weights are offered.

- Counting Tape: Several times during the month, allow students to use counters to prove the multiples that have been marked on the Counting Tape so far. Allowing them to determine why a number may be a multiple of more than one number will help in developing understanding of multiplication.

- Coin Counter: Students that catch on quickly to solving problems may enjoy making up their own *What Are My Coins?* problems. On the front of an index card, students can write, "I used ___ coins to make ___ amount." On the back they can draw or use a stamp of the coins to prove their solution. Have students solve each other's cards.

?
7 coins

Assessments

March Assessment: See pages 97–100.

Spring Test: See pages 65–68.

Multiplication Facts Progress Record: See page 112.

Assessment Checklist: See pages 109–110.

© Houghton Mifflin Harcourt Publishing Company

March Week 1

Vocabulary This Month

Growing pattern, division, remainder, balance, ounce, pound, survey, poll

Update Questions

Be sure to ask: **How many? What number? What date? What coins? How many pounds? How many hours since? How many until?**

Elements for Number of Days in School

- Counting Tape and Hundred Chart (TG p. 108 Daily Routine)
- Depositor (TG p. 110 Daily Routine)
- Coin Counter (TG p.110)

Elements for Calendar Date

- Calendar (TG p. 102 Daily Routine)
- Computations and Connections (TG p. 103 Daily Routine)
- Clock (TG p. 107 Daily Routine)

Extras This Month

- Graph (TG p. 112 Daily Routine)
- Measurement (TG p. 105 Daily Routine)

Discussion Questions

Follow up with these questions: **How do you know? How did you get your answer? How do these compare or contrast? Explain your reasoning.**

Monday	Tuesday	Wednesday	Thursday	Friday
Calendar (TG p. 102) How would you describe today's Calendar Piece? **Computations and Connections** (TG p. 104) How can I share today's amount among two pockets? Is there a remainder? **Measurement** (TG p. 106) The pound of clay is cut into 16 pieces. How much does each piece weigh? What did you use to weigh it?	**Counting Tape and Hundred Chart** (TG p. 109) How will you know if a number is a multiple of 5 and gets underlined? **Depositor** (TG p. 109) What is today's total rounded to the nearest 100? **Coin Counter** (TG p. 111) I have 7 coins that equal $1.00. What combination of coins could I have?	**Graph** (TG p. 112) What are the options in our preference poll? How will we collect our information? How many votes are represented by one square on our graph? **Clock** (TG p. 107) How many hours did the *Go Ahead Clock* and the *Go Back Clock* move? What is the time on each of the clocks? List an activity that you might be doing at the time on each of the clocks.	**Counting Tape and Hundred Chart** (TG p. 109) How many triangles have we drawn since the 100th day? How many circles? How many squares? **Depositor** (TG p. 109) Write today's amount in words and expanded notation. **Coin Counter** (TG p. 110) What is today's amount using only dimes and pennies? Only quarters and pennies?	**Calendar** (TG p. 102) What is the shape pattern? **Computations and Connections** (TG p. 104) Tell a story to match today's amount shared among two pockets. **Measurement** (TG p. 106) What is the weight in ounces today? How many pounds is that? **Clock** (TG p. 107) Tell a story that involves 5 hours of elapsed time.

TG refers to the Teacher's Guide.

© Houghton Mifflin Harcourt Publishing Company

March Week 2

Vocabulary This Month

Growing pattern, division, remainder, balance, ounce, pound, survey, poll

Update Questions

Be sure to ask: **How many? What number? What date? What coins? How many pounds? How many hours since? How many until?**

Elements for Number of Days in School

- Counting Tape and Hundred Chart (TG p. 108 Daily Routine)
- Depositor (TG p. 110 Daily Routine)
- Coin Counter (TG p.110)

Elements for Calendar Date

- Calendar (TG p. 102 Daily Routine)
- Computations and Connections (TG p. 103 Daily Routine)
- Clock (TG p. 107 Daily Routine)

Extras This Month

- Graph (TG p. 112 Daily Routine)
- Measurement (TG p. 105 Daily Routine)

Discussion Questions

Follow up with these questions: **How do you know? How did you get your answer? How do these compare or contrast? Explain your reasoning.**

Monday	Tuesday	Wednesday	Thursday	Friday
Calendar (TG p. 102) What do you notice about the purple triangles? The green squares? **Computations and Connections** (TG p. 104) Share today's amount among 2, 3, 4, or 5 pockets. Tell a story to match. **Measurement** (TG p. 106) Last month we also measured in ounces. What is the difference between the two types?	**Counting Tape and Hundred Chart** (TG p. 109) Count by 5s starting with 100. How many groups of 5 have passed since Day 100? **Depositor** (TG p. 109) Describe how you added today's amount to the total. **Coin Counter** (TG p. 111) What is today's total? Make up a *What Are My Coins?* problem using today's total amount.	**Graph** (TG p. 112) What is the most popular choice on our Graph so far? How many people have participated in our poll so far? **Clock** (TG p. 108) What will the time be in ___ hours from now? What might you be doing then? **Measurement** (TG p. 106) How many ounces equal a half-pound? Is today's weight more or less than a half-pound? By how much?	**Counting Tape and Hundred Chart** (TG p. 109) What is today's number rounded to the nearest ten? Nearest hundred? **Depositor** (TG p. 109) If we spend $1800, about how much money would be left in the Depositor? How did you get your answer? **Coin Counter** (TG p. 110) Rulers cost 27¢. How many can you buy for $1? How did you get your answer?	**Calendar** (TG p. 102) If the pattern continues, how many green squares will appear in March? **Computations and Connections** (TG p. 103) If you equally share today's amount among 4 children, how many will each child get? How many will be left over? **Clock** (TG p. 108) Look at the classroom clock. Draw a picture of what the clock will look like in 6 hours.

TG refers to the Teacher's Guide.

© Houghton Mifflin Harcourt Publishing Company

March Week 3

Vocabulary This Month

Growing pattern, division, remainder, balance, ounce, pound, survey, poll

Update Questions

Be sure to ask: **How many? What number? What date? What coins? How many pounds? How many hours since? How many until?**

Elements for Number of Days in School

- Counting Tape and Hundred Chart (TG p. 108 Daily Routine)
- Depositor (TG p. 110 Daily Routine)
- Coin Counter (TG p.110)

Elements for Calendar Date

- Calendar (TG p. 102 Daily Routine)
- Computations and Connections (TG p. 103 Daily Routine)
- Clock (TG p. 107 Daily Routine)

Extras This Month

- Graph (TG p. 112 Daily Routine)
- Measurement (TG p. 105 Daily Routine)

Discussion Questions

Follow up with these questions: **How do you know? How did you get your answer? How do these compare or contrast? Explain your reasoning.**

Monday	Tuesday	Wednesday	Thursday	Friday
Calendar (TG p. 103) How many sides are on 1 purple triangle? How many will appear over the whole month? **Measurement** (TG p. 105) How many pounds are in 26 ounces? How many extra ounces are there? **Clock** (TG p. 108) What was the time ___ hours ago? What were you doing then?	**Counting Tape and Hundred Chart** (TG p. 108) How many groups of 5 are in 40? In 50? In 32? How do you know if you will have any leftover? **Depositor** (TG p. 109) What is today's total using only hundred- and one-dollar bills? **Coin Counter** (TG p. 110) What is the total value of 1 dollar, 1 quarter, 1 dime, 1 nickel and 1 penny? Can you use different coins to make the same total?	**Graph** (TG p. 113) Do we have enough data to draw conclusions about our Graph? Why or why not? **Clock** (TG p. 43) Baseball practice started 2 hours ago and Sam is late at 1:30 P.M. What time did practice start? **Computations and Connections** (TG p. 103) Write a story to go with the division problem $15 \div 3 = ?$	**Counting Tape and Hundred Chart** (TG p. 109) How many school days have passed since Day 88? **Depositor** (TG p. 34) Which thousand is today's total closest to? What is the difference between the two numbers? **Coin Counter** (TG p. 42) Using the least number of coins, how many coins will you need to make today's total? What is another way to make today's total?	**Calendar** (TG p. 102) What fraction of this week's Calendar Pieces is green squares? **Computations and Connections** (TG p. 104) Tell a multiplication and a division story that would match today's amount. **Measurement** (TG p. 106) Can you think of anything that is as heavy as today's weight? **Clock** (TG p. 108) What is the time on all 3 clocks?

TG refers to the Teacher's Guide.

© Houghton Mifflin Harcourt Publishing Company

March Week 4

Vocabulary This Month

Growing pattern, division, remainder, balance, ounce, pound, survey, poll

Update Questions

Be sure to ask: **How many? What number? What date? What coins? How many pounds? How many hours since? How many until?**

Elements for Number of Days in School

- Counting Tape and Hundred Chart (TG p. 108 Daily Routine)
- Depositor (TG p. 110 Daily Routine)
- Coin Counter (TG p.110)

Elements for Calendar Date

- Calendar (TG p. 102 Daily Routine)
- Computations and Connections (TG p. 103 Daily Routine)
- Clock (TG p. 107 Daily Routine)

Extras This Month

- Graph (TG p. 112 Daily Routine)
- Measurement (TG p. 105 Daily Routine)

Discussion Questions

Follow up with these questions: **How do you know? How did you get your answer? How do these compare or contrast? Explain your reasoning.**

Monday	Tuesday	Wednesday	Thursday	Friday
Calendar (TG p. 102) Use the letters *A* and *B* to describe the appearance of each triangle and square in this month's pattern. **Computations and Connections** (TG p. 104) Use repeated addition to describe today's amount. Write a multiplication sentence to match. **Clock** (TG p. 107) How do you know when the clock changes from A.M. to P.M.? From P.M. to A.M.?	**Counting Tape and Hundred Chart** (TG p. 108) Explain how you would figure out how many one-dollar bills you can get for 11 five-dollar bills. **Depositor** (TG p. 109) Have you changed your estimate about reaching $1 million by the end of the year? Why or why not? **Coin Counter** (TG p. 111) I have 9 coins that equal 63¢. *What Are My Coins?*	**Graph** (TG p. 113) How many more people prefer _____ than ___? What other conclusions can you draw? **Clock** (TG p. 108) On what day were the 3 clocks exactly a day apart? Explain. **Computations and Connections** (TG p. 104) How will you know whether the amount shared will have a remainder?	**Counting Tape and Hundred Chart** (TG p. 109) What is the pattern of multiples of 5 in the ones place? Is 1,234,089 a multiple of 5? Why or why not? **Depositor** (TG p. 110) What are three amounts that will round to $8,700? **Coin Counter** (TG p. 110) If you buy an eraser for 59¢ and pay $1, how much change will you get back?	**Calendar** (TG p. 103) If you made the sides of the square with toothpicks, how many toothpicks would be on the first set of green squares? The second set? The third set? The month? **Measurement** (TG p. 106) How many pounds and ounces have we weighed today? How many ounces until our next pound? What will our total be for the month?

TG refers to the Teacher's Guide.

© Houghton Mifflin Harcourt Publishing Company

Big Math Ideas This Month

Recognize symmetrical and asymmetrical figures, explore multiples of 6, explore patterns of multiples of 10, convert capacity between milliliters and liters, add and subtract mentally, estimate with multiplication using coins

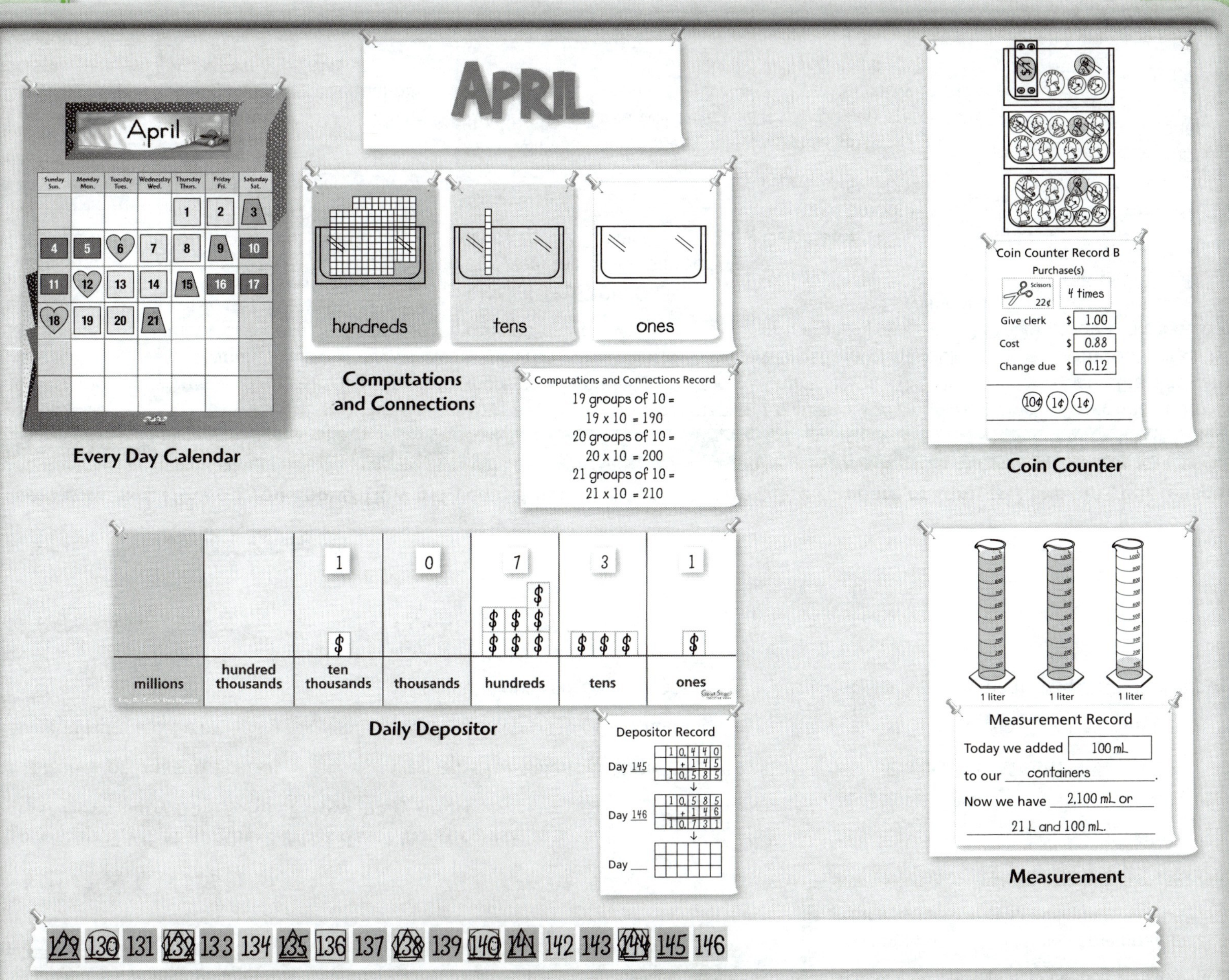

© Houghton Mifflin Harcourt Publishing Company

Monthly Resources

Intervention

- **Multiples of 10: Small Group:** Many students quickly see the pattern of adding a zero to the number when multiplying by 10, but may not conceptually understand why that works. Use bundling sticks, or other materials, to have students make collections of tens. Ask, "How many bundles do we have? How many sticks? What is our total?" Have students make 4 groups of ten. Ask, "How many groups of ten do we have? How many is that?" Continue to make "groups of" ten and comparing the groups of ten to the total number. Ask, "How many tens are in ___?"
- **Multiples of 6: Small Group:** Skip counting by 6 is a sequence that is more difficult than the previous sequences of 2s, 5s, 10s, 3s, and 4s shown on the Counting Tape. Practicing this number word sequence will help when working out problems, but will not help with understanding. Remind students that in multiplication and division relationships, there are three parts to the problem: the number of groups, the number in each group and the total. Manipulating the questions asked so that students have practice looking for each part and the whole will build fluency with the number word sequence and give them an opportunity to explore the relationships. For multiplication, provide the number of groups and the number in each group, and ask students to find the total. For partitive division, give students the total and the number of groups, and have students find the number in each group. For measurement division, given the total and the number in each group, students will find the number of groups.

138 139 140 141 142 143 144 145 146

- **Arrays: Small Group:** Arrays provide a visual for the commutative property of multiplication. Initially, multiplication is introduced as "groups of." In this scenario, 6 × 4 (6 groups of 4) would have a different pictorial representation than 4 × 6 (4 groups of 6). Have students make conclusions about the total when exploring the rows and columns of arrays. Rotate the arrays and have students count by a different multiple to find the total.

More Helpful Hints

- Calendar: Use the Calendar Pieces for a draw and replace probability experiment. Put the first 6 pieces in a bag and ask the following questions: What is the likelihood of drawing a trapezoid out of the bag? Is drawing a heart out of the bag more likely or less likely than drawing a green rectangle? Is there a greater chance of drawing a yellow square than a green rectangle, or are the chances about the same? Why?
- Computations and Connections: Make Array Cards for 6 × 10 through 9 × 10 so students can see that if they know 6 groups of 10 are 60, they also know the product for 10 groups of 6, and so on.

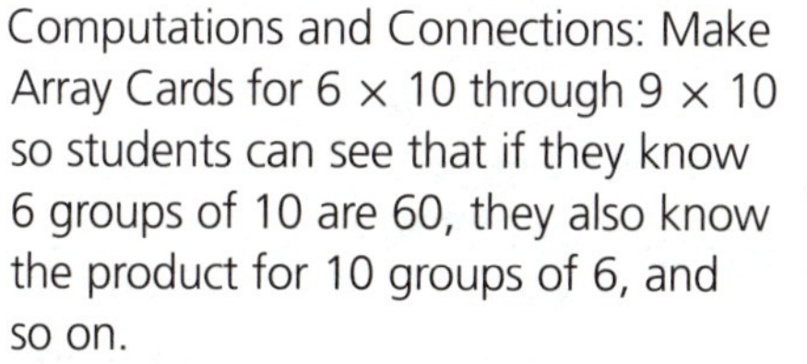

Computations and Connections Record

6 groups of 10 = 60
6 x 10 = 60

7 groups of 10 = 70
7 x 10 = 70

- Measurement: Collect containers to hold the colored water by having students bring empty liter containers from home. Be sure to have a lid for each container because evaporation affects outcome.

Assessments

April Assessment: See pages 101–104.

Spring Test: See pages 65–68.

Multiplication Facts Progress Record: See page 112.

Assessment Checklist: See pages 109–110.

© Houghton Mifflin Harcourt Publishing Company

April Week 1

Vocabulary This Month

Line of symmetry, symmetrical, asymmetrical, liter, milliliter

Update Questions

Be sure to ask: **How many? What number? What date? What coins? What multiple? How many milliliters?**

Elements for Number of Days in School

- Counting Tape and Hundred Chart (TG p. 122 Daily Routine)
- Depositor (TG p. 123 Daily Routine)
- Coin Counter (TG p. 125 Daily Routine)

Elements for Calendar Date

- Calendar (TG p. 116 Daily Routine)
- Computations and Connections (TG p. 118 Daily Routine)

Extras This Month

- Measurement (TG p. 120 Daily Routine)

Discussion Questions

Follow up with these questions: **How do you know? How did you get your answer? How do these compare or contrast? Explain your reasoning.**

Monday	Tuesday	Wednesday	Thursday	Friday
Calendar (TG p. 116) How would you describe today's Calendar Piece? **Computations and Connections** (TG p. 119) How many 10 strips do we collect each day? Describe a 10 strip as ones (10 ones). Describe a 10 strip as tens (1 ten). **Measurement** (TG p. 120) If we add 100 milliliters each day, how many days will it be until we have 1 liter?	**Counting Tape and Hundred Chart** (TG p. 122) How can you be sure that a number on the Tapes gets a hexagon? **Depositor** (TG p. 123) How would you round today's total to the nearest $100? Nearest $10? **Coin Counter** (TG p. 125) If you have only $1, how many packs of candy at 33¢ a pack can you buy? How did you get your answer?	**Calendar** (TG p. 116) Describe the square. What attribute(s) does it share with a rectangle? Which attribute(s) is different? **Computations and Connections** (TG p. 119) Count today's amount by tens. How many tens are there?	**Counting Tape and Hundred Chart** (TG p. 122) Do all the multiples of 6 already have a triangle? Describe the relationship. **Depositor** (TG p. 123) If a family's rent was $980 a month, about how many months of rent would our amount cover? **Coin Counter** (TG p. 125) I have 8 coins. They total 82¢. What are my coins?	**Calendar** (TG p. 116) Describe the trapezoid. How is it similar to a rectangle? How is it different? **Computations and Connections** (TG p. 119) How many 10 strips have we collected so far? Describe our amount as ones and as tens. **Measurement** (TG p. 120) How many milliliters do we have so far? Is that more or less than half a liter?

TG refers to the Teacher's Guide.

© Houghton Mifflin Harcourt Publishing Company

April Week 2

Vocabulary This Month

Line of symmetry, symmetrical, asymmetrical, liter, milliliter

Update Questions

Be sure to ask: **How many? What number? What date? What coins? What multiple? How many milliliters?**

Elements for Number of Days in School

- Counting Tape and Hundred Chart (TG p. 122 Daily Routine)
- Depositor (TG p. 123 Daily Routine)
- Coin Counter (TG p. 125 Daily Routine)

Elements for Calendar Date

- Calendar (TG p. 116 Daily Routine)
- Computations and Connections (TG p. 118 Daily Routine)

Extras This Month

- Measurement (TG p. 120 Daily Routine)

Discussion Questions

Follow up with these questions: **How do you know? How did you get your answer? How do these compare or contrast? Explain your reasoning.**

Monday	Tuesday	Wednesday	Thursday	Friday
Calendar (TG p. 116) What is this month's shape pattern? Can you predict what shape will be on the 19th Calendar Piece? The 24th? **Computations and Connections** (TG p. 119) How many 10 strips make 100? So how many tens is that? **Measurement** (TG p. 120) How many milliliters are in 2 liters?	**Counting Tape and Hundred Chart** (TG p. 122) How can we round today's number to the nearest ten? Hundred? Thousand? **Depositor** (TG p. 124) How would you make today's amount using thousands, hundreds, tens and ones? **Coin Counter** (TG p. 125) What is today's amount using the fewest amount of coins? What is another way to make today's amount?	**Calendar** (TG p. 117) Which shapes have at least one line of symmetry? Which shapes have no line of symmetry and therefore are asymmetrical? How do you know? How can you show us? **Coin Counter** (TG p. 125) I have 12 coins. They total $1.12. What are my coins?	**Counting Tape and Hundred Chart** (TG p. 122) Can you use the "greater than" symbol to order today's number and 2 other numbers from greatest to least? **Depositor** (TG p. 124) What is the value of the digit ___ in today's total? **Coin Counter** (TG p. 125) If you buy 2 packs of crayons at 42¢ each and pay with $1, what will your change be?	**Calendar** (TG p. 116) In your own words, describe what makes a figure symmetrical. **Computations and Connections** (TG p. 119) How many tens do we have so far? How many ones is that? How many hundreds is that? **Measurement** (TG p. 121) How many liters have we filled so far? How many extra milliliters are there?

TG refers to the Teacher's Guide.

© Houghton Mifflin Harcourt Publishing Company

April Week 3

Vocabulary This Month

Line of symmetry, symmetrical, asymmetrical, liter, milliliter

Update Questions

Be sure to ask: **How many? What number? What date? What coins? What multiple? How many milliliters?**

Elements for Number of Days in School

- Counting Tape and Hundred Chart (TG p. 122 Daily Routine)
- Depositor (TG p. 123 Daily Routine)
- Coin Counter (TG p. 125 Daily Routine)

Elements for Calendar Date

- Calendar (TG p. 116 Daily Routine)
- Computations and Connections (TG p. 118 Daily Routine)

Extras This Month

- Measurement (TG p. 120 Daily Routine)

Discussion Questions

Follow up with these questions: **How do you know? How did you get your answer? How do these compare or contrast? Explain your reasoning.**

Monday	Tuesday	Wednesday	Thursday	Friday
Calendar (TG p. 117) What dates are on the trapezoids? The hearts? How are these numbers related? **Computations and Connections** (TG p. 119) Tell a story that matches the amount we have today. **Measurement** (TG p. 120) If we continue to add 100 milliliters each day, how many will we have at the end of the month?	**Counting Tape and Hundred Chart** (TG p. 122) How many hexagons are there up to 60? To 120? How many since Day 120? **Depositor** (TG p. 124) What if we spent ___ on ___. How much money would we have left? **Coin Counter** (TG p. 125) I have 11 coins. They total 55¢. What are my coins?	**Calendar** (TG p. 117) What will the date be on the last trapezoid? The last heart? **Depositor** (TG p. 124) Have you changed your estimate for how much money you think we will collect by the end of the year? Explain.	**Counting Tape and Hundred Chart** (TG p. 122) How many numbers have squares so far? Do any of those also have hexagons? What does that mean? **Depositor** (TG p. 124) How can we write today's amount in expanded notation? **Coin Counter** (TG p. 125) If you have a dollar bill, what is the least number of coins you still need to have $1.46?	**Calendar** (TG p. 117) Which shapes have more than one line of symmetry? What do you observe about those shapes? **Computations and Connections** (TG p. 119) How can we count our amount by ones? By tens? By hundreds? **Measurement** (TG p. 120) How many liters is 3,000 milliliters?

TG refers to the Teacher's Guide.

© Houghton Mifflin Harcourt Publishing Company

April Week 4

Vocabulary This Month

Line of symmetry, symmetrical, asymmetrical, liter, milliliter

Update Questions

Be sure to ask: **How many? What number? What date? What coins? What multiple? How many milliliters?**

Elements for Number of Days in School

- Counting Tape and Hundred Chart (TG p. 122 Daily Routine)
- Depositor (TG p. 123 Daily Routine)
- Coin Counter (TG p. 125 Daily Routine)

Elements for Calendar Date

- Calendar (TG p. 116 Daily Routine)
- Computations and Connections (TG p. 118 Daily Routine)

Extras This Month

- Measurement (TG p. 120 Daily Routine)

Discussion Questions

Follow up with these questions: **How do you know? How did you get your answer? How do these compare or contrast? Explain your reasoning.**

Monday	Tuesday	Wednesday	Thursday	Friday
Calendar (TG p. 116) What fraction of the first six Calendar Pieces are squares? **Computations and Connections** (TG p. 118) How many tens are in 40? In 140? In 240? **Measurement** (TG p. 120) Is a milliliter about the same as a quart? How do you know?	**Counting Tape and Hundred Chart** (TG p. 121) How many groups of 6 can be made from 32? How many are left? **Depositor** (TG p. 124) Will we be able to trade for another $10,000 bill before the end of the school year? Why or why not? **Coin Counter** (TG p. 125) Write a *What are My Coins* problem that has a total of $1.	**Calendar** (TG p. 117) Remembering that squares are also rectangles, what fraction of the pieces are rectangles? **Computations and Connections** (TG p. 119) How can we predict what 34 times 10 will be? What about 50 times 10? How do you know?	**Counting Tape and Hundred Chart** (TG p. 122) Which numbers are multiples of 3 or more numbers? Write a multiplication sentence that describes one. **Depositor** (TG p. 124) How can we estimate today's total to the nearest thousand? **Coin Counter** (TG p. 125) Choose a Shopper Card. How many of that item could you buy using today's total amount?	**Calendar** (TG p. 117) Describe this month's pattern using the attributes of symmetrical and asymmetrical. What other ways could you describe the pattern? **Measurement** (TG p. 120) What kind of liquids might you measure with milliliters? What items could you buy that might come in liters?

TG refers to the Teacher's Guide.

© Houghton Mifflin Harcourt Publishing Company

Big Math Ideas This Month

Examine real objects as three-dimensional shapes; explore multiples of 7, 8, 9; understand inverse relationship of multiplication and division; connect division and fractions; collect, organize and analyze weather data in a bar graph

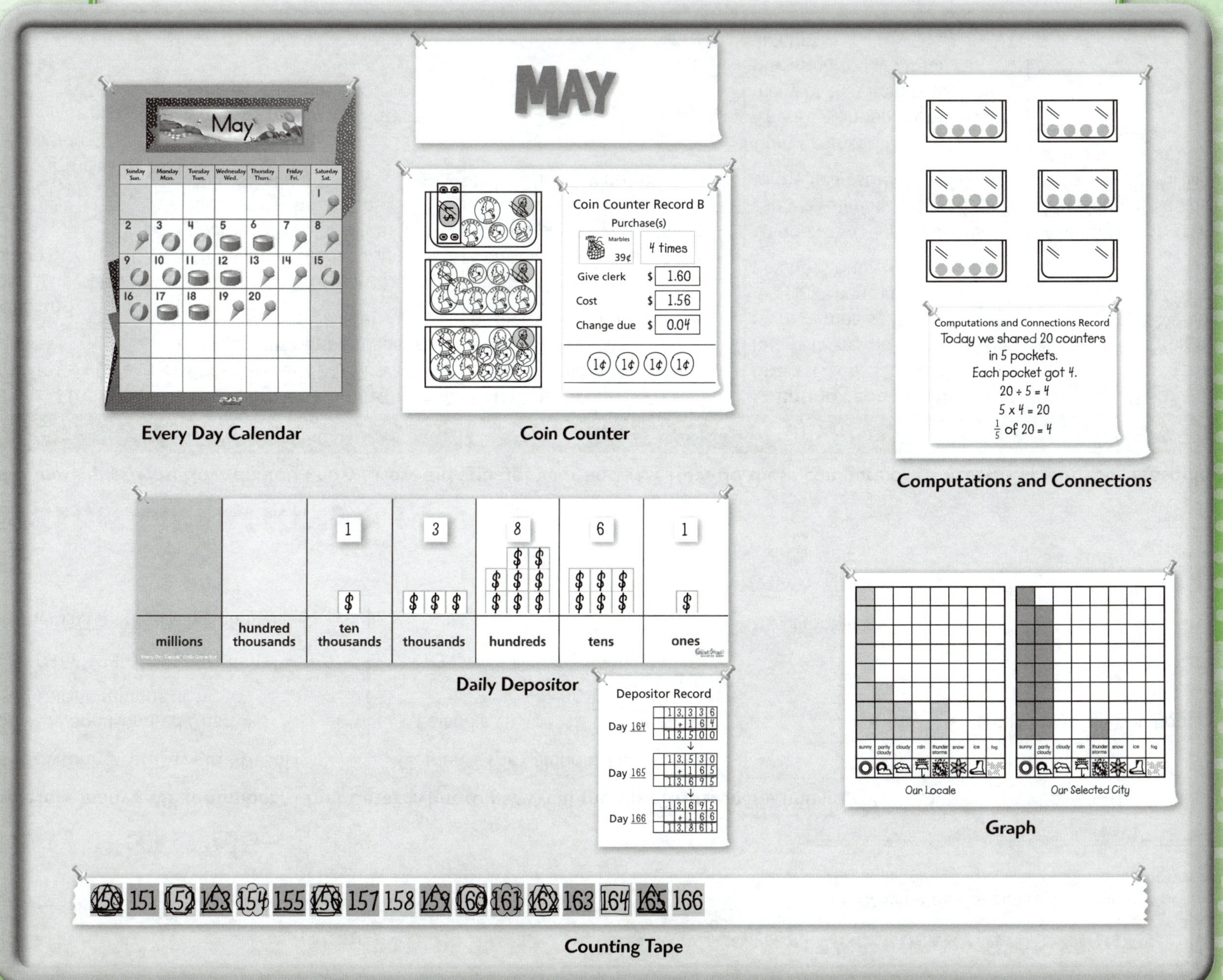

Every Day Calendar

Coin Counter

Computations and Connections

Daily Depositor

Graph

Counting Tape

© Houghton Mifflin Harcourt Publishing Company

Monthly Resources

Intervention

- **Division: Small Group:** Review division as a relationship of three parts: the total number of items, the number of groups the items are broken into, and the number of items in each group. Give students opportunities to try out different division problems.
  For partitive division, give students the total and the number of groups, and have students find the number in each group.
  For measurement division, give students the total and the number in each group, students will find the number of groups. It is not necessary to have students distinguish between the two, but it is important to expose them to the language of each and to the writing of number sentences. Allow students to use manipulatives to act out story problems and encourage them to create their own. Also provide opportunities for the items in the group and/or the groups to be hidden so that students begin to create mental images of the amounts and find ways other than using the manipulatives to count the totals. Finally, have students explore the relationship between multiplication, division and the fraction that can be written about each part.

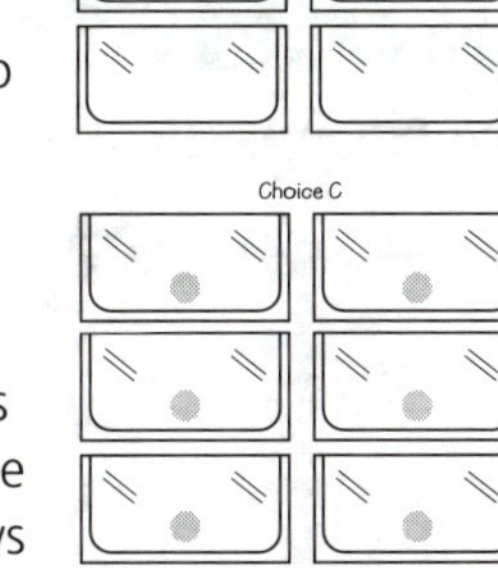

- **Renaming with Money: Small Group:**
  Using money from the Depositor, allow students to explore different combinations of money to represent the same amount. Because the Depositor is based on our Base 10 system (no $5 bills or $20 bills), renaming amounts by trading for different combinations of bills leads to a greater understanding of place value.

More Helpful Hints

- Calendar: If your school year extends into June, encourage students to work in groups to create a class pattern for the Calendar. Mount different patterns around the room and have students make predictions and observations about the different Calendar patterns.
- Counting Tape: Have students roll up their cut segments of the Counting Tape and take them to recess. Ask questions about the Counting Tape and have students stand if their segment contains the numerical answer. (e.g. Who has the number that equals 3 groups of 7? Stand if you have a multiple of 8. Who has the total of a quarter and a dime? Stand if you have 139 and 12 more. Etc.) Tell students when you blow the whistle they must line up with their segments in order from least to greatest.

  154 155 156 157 158 159 160 161 162 163 164 165 166

- Depositor: Create charts labeled *\$0–\$100*, another *\$101–\$1,000*, a third *\$1,001–\$10,000*, a fourth *\$10,001–\$100,000* and a fifth *More than \$100,000*. Challenge students to collect pictures or ads of items in real life that can be attached to the charts and arranged by how much they cost. Students may be surprised to see that while $16,000 is a great deal of money, it does not go very far when it comes to purchasing something like a house.

Assessments

May/June Assessment: See pages 105–108.

Post Test: See pages 69–72.

Multiplication Facts Progress Record: See page 112.

Assessment Checklist: See pages 109–110.

© Houghton Mifflin Harcourt Publishing Company

May/June Week 1

Vocabulary This Month

Review previous vocabulary: cone, sphere, cylinder, face, base, multiple, remainder

Update Questions

Be sure to ask: **How many? What number? What date? What coins? What multiple? What temperature?**

Elements for Number of Days in School

- Counting Tape and Hundred Chart (TG p. 132 Daily Routine)
- Depositor (TG p. 133 Daily Routine)
- Coin Counter (TG p. 134 Daily Routine)

Elements for Calendar Date

- Calendar (TG p. 128 Daily Routine)
- Computations and Connections (TG p. 130 Daily Routine)

Extras This Month

- Graph (TG p. 135 Daily Routine)

Discussion Questions

Follow up with these questions: **How do you know? How did you get your answer? How do these compare or contrast? Explain your reasoning.**

Monday	Tuesday	Wednesday	Thursday	Friday
Calendar (TG p. 128) What pictures are shown on the Calendar so far? What shapes do they represent? **Computations and Connections** (TG p. 131) How many counters will you share today? How will you share them?	**Counting Tape and Hundred Chart** (TG p. 132) What odd-numbered days are between Day 150 and today? Which ones are multiples of 3? **Depositor** (TG p. 133) What is today's total rounded to the nearest 100? Nearest 1,000? Nearest 10,000? **Coin Counter** (TG p. 134) One ruler costs 27¢. What is a good estimate of the cost of 3 rulers?	**Graph** (TG p. 135) Based on our data so far, how do you think our weather in May will compare to our selected city's weather in May? Will the weather be similar or different? **Calendar** (TG p. 128) How would you describe a cylinder? Does it have a flat base? Does it roll? Can you stack cylinders?	**Counting Tape and Hundred Chart** (TG p. 132) What are the first five multiples of 7? What are the first five multiples of 8? What do you notice about the distance between multiples as the numbers increase? **Depositor** (TG p. 133) How much do we need to get to the next hundred dollars? How did you get your answer?	**Calendar (TG p. 128)** How would you describe a cone? Does it have a flat base? Does it roll? Can you stack cones? **Computations and Connections** (TG p. 131) How could you share the counters today? Is there another way? **Coin Counter** (TG p. 134) How could you make today's amount using only coins?

TG refers to the Teacher's Guide.

© Houghton Mifflin Harcourt Publishing Company

May/June Week 2

Vocabulary This Month

Review previous vocabulary: cone, sphere, cylinder, face, base, multiple, remainder

Update Questions

Be sure to ask: **How many? What number? What date? What coins? What multiple? What temperature?**

Elements for Number of Days in School

- Counting Tape and Hundred Chart (TG p. 132 Daily Routine)
- Depositor (TG p. 133 Daily Routine)
- Coin Counter (TG p. 134 Daily Routine)

Elements for Calendar Date

- Calendar (TG p. 128 Daily Routine)
- Computations and Connections (TG p. 130 Daily Routine)

Extras This Month

- Graph (TG p. 135 Daily Routine)

Discussion Questions

Follow up with these questions: **How do you know? How did you get your answer? How do these compare or contrast? Explain your reasoning.**

Monday	Tuesday	Wednesday	Thursday	Friday
Calendar (TG p. 128) What is the shape pattern? How are these shapes alike? How are they different? **Computations and Connections** (TG p. 131) Share today's total equally among some pockets. What is your total number of counters? How many groups? How many in each group?	**Counting Tape and Hundred Chart** (TG p. 132) What is today's number rounded to the nearest 10? Nearest 100? **Depositor** (TG p. 133) How much money would we have left if we spent \$10,000? \$1,000? **Coin Counter** (TG p. 134) How can we show today's amount with the least amount of coins? Give two other combinations.	**Graph** (TG p. 135) What kind of weather has our selected city had forecast most often? How does this compare to the weather there in October? January? **Coin Counter** (TG p. 134) If you shared today's amount with 3 other people, how much would each person get? How many people were there? Was there any money left?	**Counting Tape and Hundred Chart** (TG p. 132) How many octagons are there up to 100? What numbers are inside the octagons? **Depositor** (TG p. 133) How could you make today's total using only \$10 bills and \$1 bills? **Coin Counter** (TG p. 134) How many sets of jacks at 25¢ can you buy with today's total? How much change would you receive?	**Calendar** (TG p. 128) If the pattern continues, what picture will be on the last day in May? **Computations and Connections** (TG p. 131) Tell a multiplication story that matches the way the counters are shared. Tell a division story that matches the way the counters are shared.

TG refers to the Teacher's Guide.

© Houghton Mifflin Harcourt Publishing Company

May/June Week 3

Vocabulary This Month

Review previous vocabulary: cone, sphere, cylinder, face, base, multiple, remainder

Update Questions

Be sure to ask: **How many? What number? What date? What coins? What multiple? What temperature?**

Elements for Number of Days in School

- Counting Tape and Hundred Chart (TG p. 132 Daily Routine)
- Depositor (TG p. 133 Daily Routine)
- Coin Counter (TG p. 134 Daily Routine)

Elements for Calendar Date

- Calendar (TG p. 128 Daily Routine)
- Computations and Connections (TG p. 130 Daily Routine)

Extras This Month

- Graph (TG p. 135 Daily Routine)

Discussion Questions

Follow up with these questions: **How do you know? How did you get your answer? How do these compare or contrast? Explain your reasoning.**

Monday	Tuesday	Wednesday	Thursday	Friday
Calendar (TG p. 129) What makes a cylinder different from a cone? A sphere? **Computations and Connections** (TG p. 131) How can today's total be shared equally among some pockets? Share the same total among some pockets so that there is a remainder. Write a number sentence for each.	**Counting Tape and Hundred Chart** (TG p. 132) How many groups of 4 are in today's number? Are there any extras? On what day will the next multiple of 4 appear? **Depositor** (TG p. 133) How close are we to $10,000? To $100,000? To $1,000,000? **Coin Counter** (TG p. 134) What is today's amount rounded to the nearest dollar?	**Graph** (TG p. 135) In our sample, how many more (or fewer) sunny days have been forecast this month at home than in our selected city? **Counting Tape** (TG p. 132) How many flowers (multiples of 7) are there up to 100? What numbers are inside the flowers? Where is the 7th flower? The 9th flower? Is it 7 less than the 10th flower? Explain.	**Counting Tape and Hundred Chart** (TG p. 132) How many days have we counted since Day 120? How did you figure that out? **Depositor** (TG p. 133) How do we write today's total in expanded form? In standard form? **Coin Counter** (TG p. 134) What coins would you use to make today's amount if you had no dimes?	**Calendar** (TG p. 129) If the pattern continues, how many pairs of cones will there be? Are there any extras? **Computations and Connections** (TG p. 119) Share today's total equally among some pockets. What is your total number of counters? How many groups? How many in each group? What is the fractional representation of one pocket?

TG refers to the Teacher's Guide.

© Houghton Mifflin Harcourt Publishing Company

May/June Week 4

Vocabulary This Month

Review previous vocabulary: cone, sphere, cylinder, face, base, multiple, remainder

Update Questions

Be sure to ask: **How many? What number? What date? What coins? What multiple? What temperature?**

Elements for Number of Days in School

- Counting Tape and Hundred Chart (TG p. 132 Daily Routine)
- Depositor (TG p. 133 Daily Routine)
- Coin Counter (TG p. 134 Daily Routine)

Elements for Calendar Date

- Calendar (TG p. 128 Daily Routine)
- Computations and Connections (TG p. 130 Daily Routine)

Extras This Month

- Graph (TG p. 135 Daily Routine)

Discussion Questions

Follow up with these questions: **How do you know? How did you get your answer? How do these compare or contrast? Explain your reasoning.**

Monday	Tuesday	Wednesday	Thursday	Friday
Calendar (TG p. 128) Can you stack a sphere? Why or why not? **Computations and Connections** (TG p. 130) What is the fraction name for one group out of four equal groups?	**Counting Tape and Hundred Chart** (TG p. 132) Mark the multiples of 9 with an arrow. What is the relationship between the multiples of 9 and the multiples of 10? **Depositor** (TG p. 133) How much money will we have by the end of the year? How close is your estimate to that amount? **Coin Counter** (TG p. 134) If a chocolate bar costs $2, how much more money would you need to buy it?	**Graph** (TG p. 135) What can you observe about the weather on the two cities' graphs? How does the weather compare to October's weather? January's weather? **Computations and Connections** (TG p. 131) Which totals this month can be shared only two ways? Describe the common ways they can be shared.	**Counting Tape and Hundred Chart** (TG p. 132) How can we cut the Counting Tape so that each student gets an equal segment? How many numerals will each student get? Will there be any numerals leftover? **Depositor** (TG p. 133) What different strategies could we use to compute the last day's amount? What could we purchase with this amount?	**Calendar** (TG p. 129) Which of these shapes can you find most often in real life? Why do you think that is the case? **Computations and Connections** (TG p. 130) Make a list showing all the ways you can share 12 counters equally so there are no leftovers. **Coin Counter** (TG p. 134) List as many ways as you can to make today's amount.

TG refers to the Teacher's Guide.

© Houghton Mifflin Harcourt Publishing Company

Assessments

© Houghton Mifflin Harcourt Publishing Company

PRETEST

NAME ______________________________

Directions: Write your answer to each question.

1. What are the next three shapes in this pattern?

____ ____ ____

2. How many equal sides does this triangle have? ________

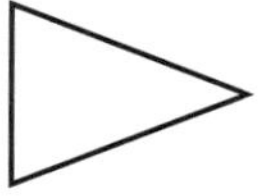

3. What fraction of this circle is shaded? ________

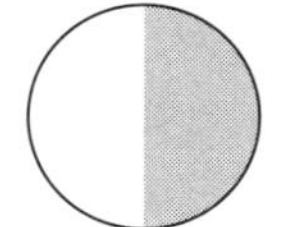

4. Sela took 5 pictures of her sister. She took 6 pictures of her brother. Write a number sentence that tells how many pictures Sela took in all.

____

5. Complete each number sentence. $4 \times$ ________ $= 24$

$6 \times$ ________ $= 24$

6. Divide. $63 \div 7 =$ ________

7. Write a multiplication sentence to tell how many buttons there are in all.

____

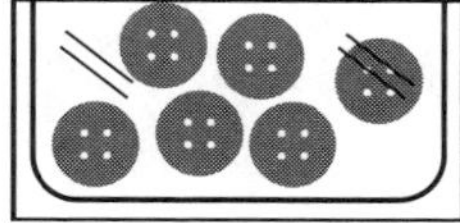

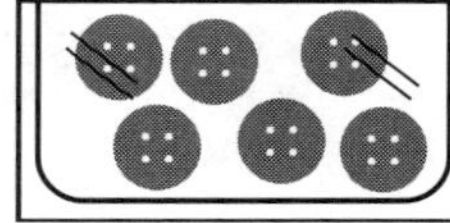

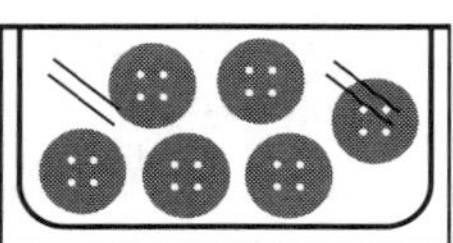

8. Add.

$$\begin{array}{r} 81 \\ +14 \\ \hline \end{array}$$

© Houghton Mifflin Harcourt Publishing Company

NAME 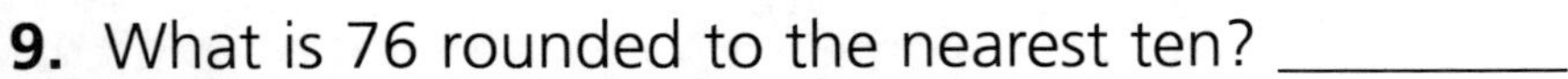

9. What is 76 rounded to the nearest ten? ________

10. Write $<$ or $>$ to make each expression true.

36 ________ 61   99 ________ 61

11. A desk is 80 centimeters wide. How many decimeters is that? ________

12. A bucket holds 48 cups of water. How many quarts is that? ________

13. To measure the length of your little finger, should you use feet or inches? ________

14. Look at the square. What is the perimeter of the square? ________

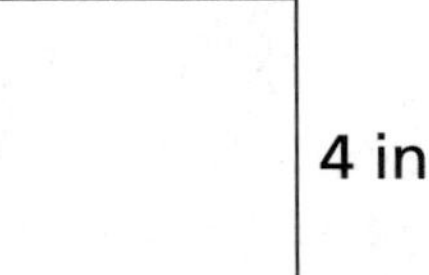

15. How many minutes are in $\frac{1}{2}$ hour? ________

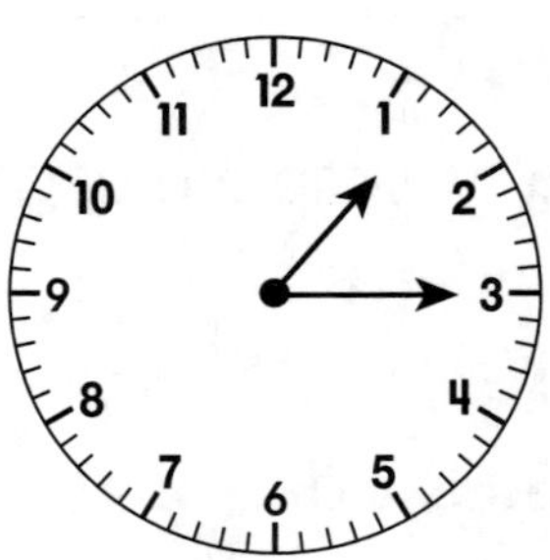

16. What time does this clock show? ________

17. What is the value of these coins? ________

18. What number is 10,000 + 3,000 + 80 + 5? Write the number.

____

© Houghton Mifflin Harcourt Publishing Company

NAME ______________________________

Directions: Choose the best answer to each question. Mark your answer.

19. In which group are all the numbers even?

Ⓐ 2, 3, 4, 5　Ⓑ 2, 4, 6, 8　Ⓒ 2, 5, 8, 11　Ⓓ 2, 6, 9, 13

20. Which of these is a square?

Ⓐ 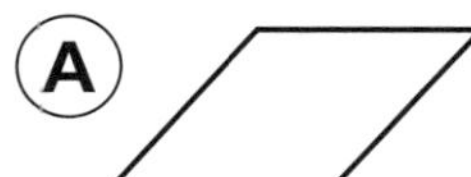　Ⓑ 　Ⓒ 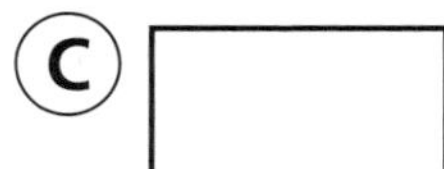　Ⓓ 

21. Which of these is a cylinder?

Ⓑ 

22. What number sentence goes with this Blank Hundred Chart?

Ⓐ $63 - 37 = 26$

Ⓑ $100 + 37 = 137$

Ⓒ $63 + 37 = 100$

Ⓓ $163 - 63 = 100$

23. What is the value of the **6** in 3,2**6**4?

Ⓐ 6　Ⓑ 60　Ⓒ 600　Ⓓ 6,000

24. How many hundreds are there in 320?

Ⓐ 32　Ⓑ 3　Ⓒ 23　Ⓓ 20

© Houghton Mifflin Harcourt Publishing Company

NAME ______________________________

25. Third graders made this graph to show which season is their favorite. Which season was picked by the most third graders?

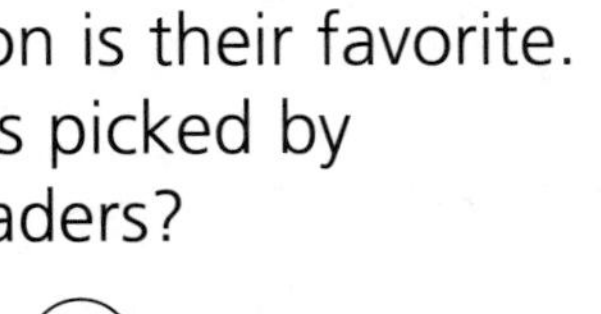

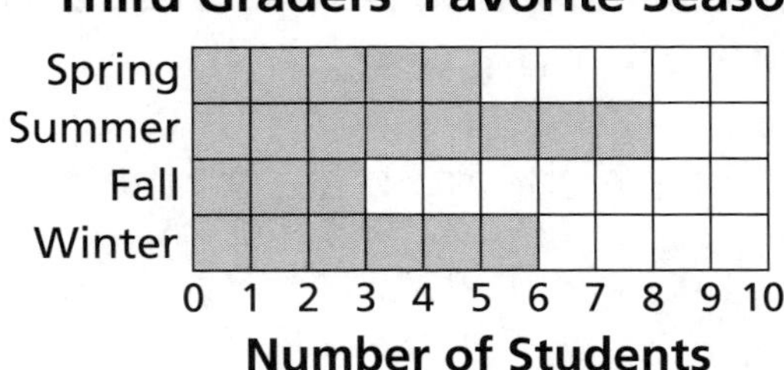

Ⓐ spring Ⓒ fall

Ⓑ summer Ⓓ winter

26. The chart shows how many times four friends flipped a coin. Which friend probably came closest to flipping half heads and half tails?

Ⓐ Liu

Ⓑ Bridget

Ⓒ Dawn

Ⓓ Joey

Name	Number of Flips
Liu	54
Bridget	70
Dawn	22
Joey	100

27. Mrs. Charles put some cookies in the oven at 4:40. If the cookies take 20 minutes to bake, what time will they be done?

Ⓐ 5:00 Ⓑ 5:10 Ⓒ 5:20 Ⓓ 6:00

28. A toy airplane costs 49¢. If Kim pays for the airplane with one dollar, how much change should she get back?

Ⓐ 61¢ Ⓑ 51¢ Ⓒ 41¢ Ⓓ 31¢

29. Vick has two dollars, three quarters, and a dime. How much money is that?

Ⓐ \$2.31 Ⓑ \$2.60 Ⓒ \$2.75 Ⓓ \$2.85

30. Dylan reads for 32 minutes on Monday. He reads for 27 minutes on Tuesday and 43 minutes on Wednesday. About how many minutes does he read in all?

Ⓐ 60 Ⓑ 80 Ⓒ 100 Ⓓ 120

© Houghton Mifflin Harcourt Publishing Company

WINTER TEST

NAME ______________________________

Directions: Write your answer to each question.

1. What are the next three numbers in this pattern?

3, 6, 9, ________, ________, ________

2. What are the next three figures in this pattern?

○ □ △ ○ □ ____ ____ ____

3. Draw a circle around each even number.

23 24 25 26 27 28 29

4. Tell two ways these figures are alike.

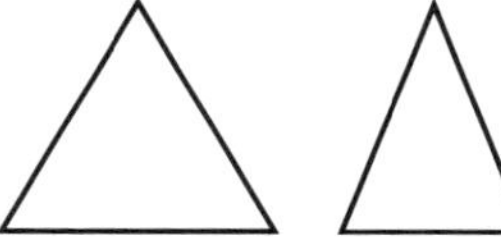

____

____

5. Write the missing numbers to show a "doubles plus one" fact.

________ + ________ = 13

6. Uma had 24 comic books. She gave 9 of the comic books to a friend. Write a number sentence to show how many comic books Uma has now.

____

7. Lee had 18 toy aliens. Then he bought some more aliens. Now he has 35 aliens. How many did he buy? ________

8. Mindy's kitchen is 300 centimeters wide. How many meters is that? ________

© Houghton Mifflin Harcourt Publishing Company

NAME ______________________________

9. What number goes in the box to complete this number sentence?

29 + ☐ = 56 __________

10. How many tens are there in 73? __________

11. Brenna wants to read 100 pages of her book this week. So far, she has read 47 pages. How many more pages does Brenna want to read?

____

12. This chart shows how many bikes Mr. Tan fixed in one week. Fill in the grid to make a graph showing how many bikes Mr. Tan fixed each day.

Day	Number of Bikes Fixed
Monday	5
Tuesday	4
Wednesday	3
Thursday	4
Friday	5

13. A door is 78 inches tall. What is the height of the door in feet?

____

14. How can you make 49¢ using the fewest coins?

____

Use the clock to answer questions 15 and 16.

15. What time does the clock show? __________

16. What time was it 15 minutes before the time shown on the clock? __________

17. How many minutes are there in $\frac{1}{4}$ hour? __________

© Houghton Mifflin Harcourt Publishing Company

NAME ______________________________

Directions: Choose the best answer to each question. Mark your answer.

18. Which figure is a trapezoid?

  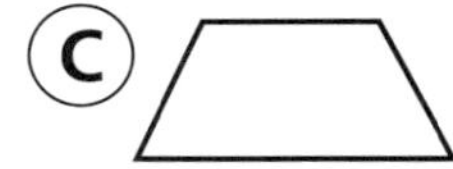 

19. What number sentence goes with this Blank Hundred Chart?

Ⓐ 23 + 77 = 100

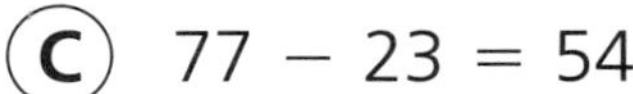
Ⓑ 100 + 23 = 123

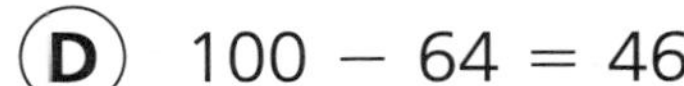
Ⓒ 77 − 23 = 54

Ⓓ 100 − 64 = 46

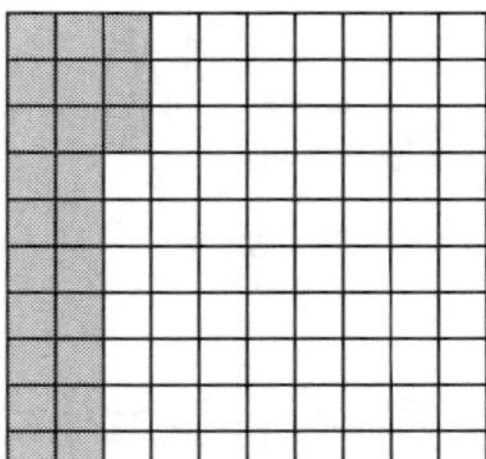

20. What is the value of the **5** in 1,**5**74?

Ⓐ 5,000 Ⓑ 500 Ⓒ 50 Ⓓ 5

21. What is 218 rounded to the nearest ten?

Ⓐ 200 Ⓑ 210 Ⓒ 220 Ⓓ 300

22. A bag holds 5 red tiles and 5 green tiles. Gina takes a tile from the bag, records the color, and puts the tile back in the bag. If Gina does this 50 times in all, which is closest to the record Gina will have when she is done?

Ⓐ 25 red, 25 green Ⓒ 5 red, 40 green

Ⓑ 15 red, 35 green Ⓓ 35 red, 15 green

23. Which is the best estimate of the length of your bed?

Ⓐ 7 yards Ⓑ 700 inches Ⓒ 7 feet Ⓓ 70 yards

© Houghton Mifflin Harcourt Publishing Company

NAME ______________________________

24. About how many inches long is this pencil?

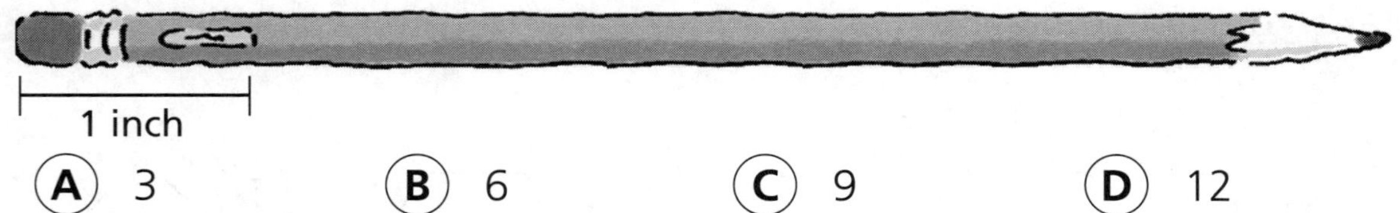

Ⓐ 3 Ⓑ 6 Ⓒ 9 Ⓓ 12

25. Which clock shows 4:50?

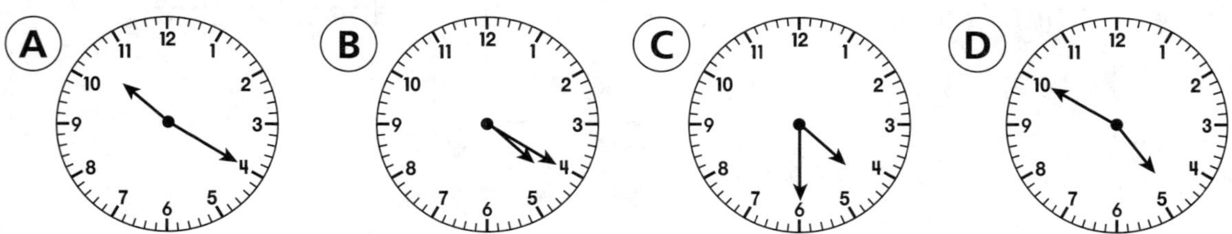

26. If it is 8:00 P.M. now and Al ate dinner two hours ago, what time did Al eat dinner?

Ⓐ 6:00 A.M. Ⓑ 10:00 A.M. Ⓒ 6:00 P.M. Ⓓ 10:00 P.M.

27. What is the value of these coins?

Ⓐ $1.12 Ⓑ $1.22 Ⓒ $1.17 Ⓓ $1.27

28. Look at the number pattern: 5, 10, 15, 20, 25, ...
If the pattern continues, what will the ninth number be?

Ⓐ 35 Ⓑ 40 Ⓒ 45 Ⓓ 50

29. Mrs. Naylor arranges the desks in her classroom in groups of two. There are 15 boys and 17 girls in the class. How many groups of two desks will there be?

Ⓐ 15 Ⓑ 16 Ⓒ 17 Ⓓ 18

30. Ted has 19 baseball cards, Laurie has 32 cards, and Lan has 28 cards. About how many cards do the friends have altogether?

Ⓐ 60 Ⓑ 80 Ⓒ 100 Ⓓ 120

© Houghton Mifflin Harcourt Publishing Company

SPRING TEST

NAME ______________________________

Directions: Write your answer to each question.

1. What are the next three numbers in this pattern?

6, 12, 18, 24, ________, ________, ________

2. What fraction of this circle is shaded? ______________

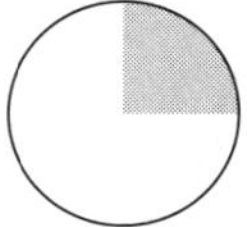

3. Will has 2 boxes of crayons. There are 8 crayons in each box. Write a multiplication sentence to find how many crayons there are in all.

____

4. How many minutes are there in one hour? ______________

5. Complete each number sentence. $4 \times$ ________ $= 36$

$9 \times$ ________ $= 36$

6. A movie starts at 7:45 and lasts 2 hours. What time will the movie end?

____

7. A pitcher holds 12 cups of juice. How many quarts of juice does the pitcher hold? ______________

8. What is 87 rounded to the nearest ten? ______________

9. Write $<$ or $>$ to make each expression true.

83 ________ 54   32 ________ 54

10. Circle each number that is a multiple of 4.

8 10 12 14 16 18 20

© Houghton Mifflin Harcourt Publishing Company

NAME ____

11. What number is 8,000 + 300 + 9? Write the number. ____________

12. Write 4,251 in expanded notation. ______________________________

13. What is the value of these coins? ____________

14. Nick bought an apple for 37¢. He paid for it with one dollar. How much change should Nick get back? ____________

15. Latoya needs 89¢ for stamps. She finds 2 quarters, 1 dime, and 3 pennies in her pocket. How much more money does Latoya need? ____________

16. The chart shows how many animals Juan saw at the pond. Fill in the grid to make a graph showing how many of each animal Juan saw.

Animal	Number Seen
Fish	4
Duck	6
Turtle	1
Beaver	2

Animals Seen at the Pond

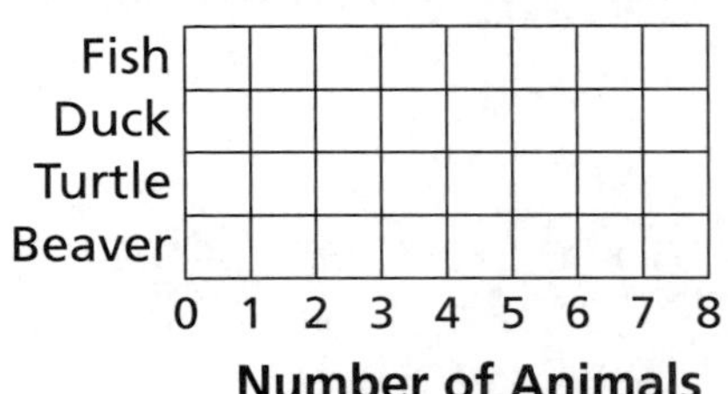

Use the graph to answer questions 17 and 18.

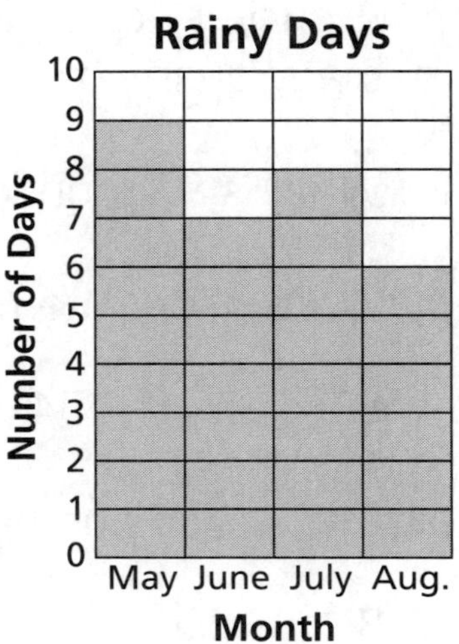

17. The graph shows how many rainy days there were in May, June, July, and August. Which month had the fewest rainy days?

____

18. How many rainy days were there in June?

____

© Houghton Mifflin Harcourt Publishing Company

NAME ______________________________

Directions: Choose the best answer to each question. Mark your answer.

19. Which shape can be made by combining these two shapes?

Ⓐ 
Ⓑ 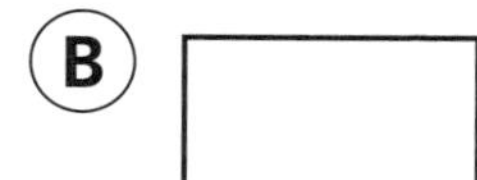
Ⓒ 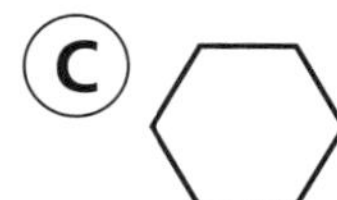
Ⓓ 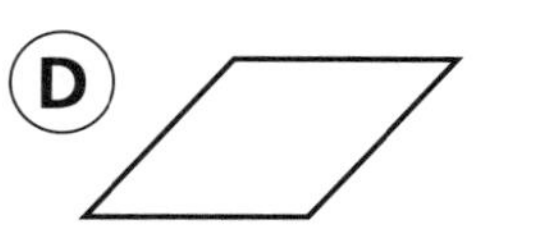

20. Which figure is a sphere?

Ⓐ 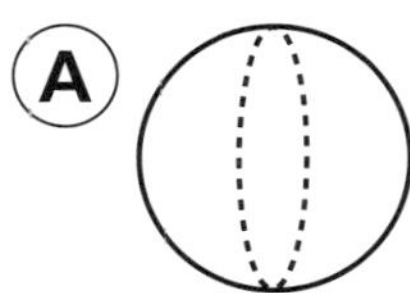
Ⓑ 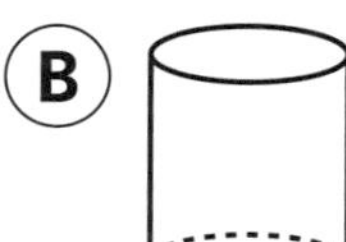
Ⓒ 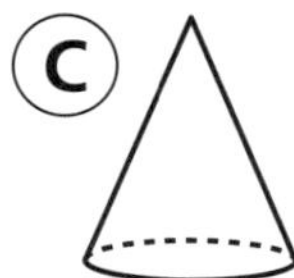
Ⓓ 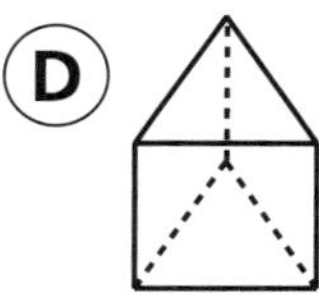

21. Which number sentence is shown by this picture?

Ⓐ $3 \times 3 = 9$

Ⓒ $3 \times 4 = 12$

Ⓑ $4 \times 2 = 8$

Ⓓ $4 \times 4 = 16$

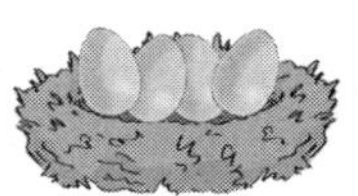
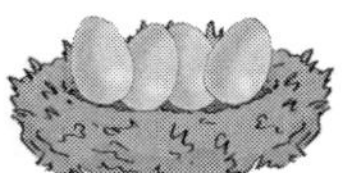
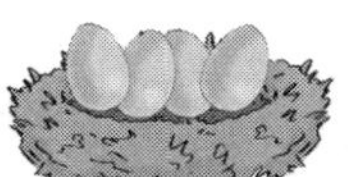

22. Which clock shows 3:45?

Ⓐ 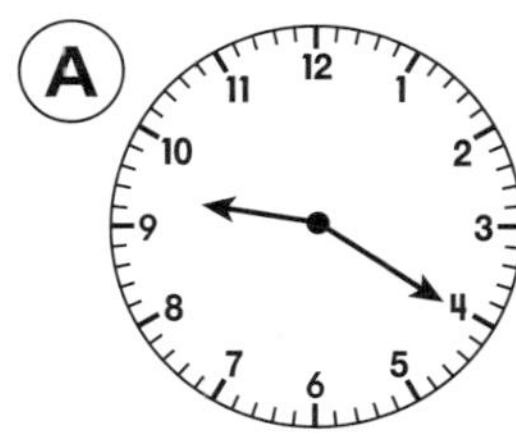
Ⓑ 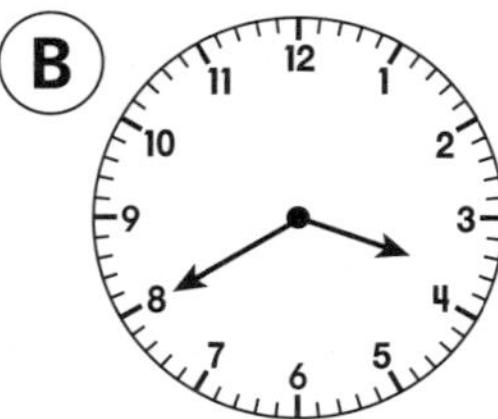
Ⓒ 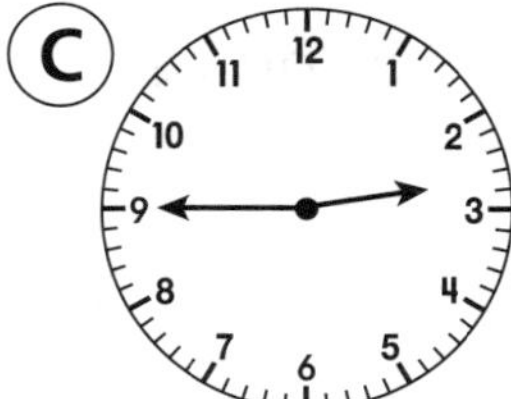
Ⓓ 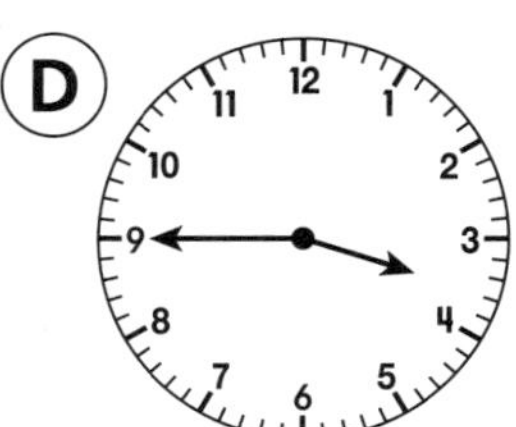

23. The squares in this figure measure one unit on each side. What is the perimeter of this figure?

Ⓐ 5 units

Ⓒ 20 units

Ⓑ 10 units

Ⓓ 50 units

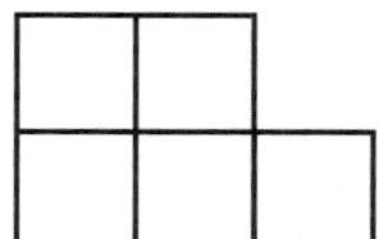

24. Jen poured 2 cups of water into the jar. About how much more water is needed to fill the jar?

Ⓐ 1 cup

Ⓒ 6 cups

Ⓑ 3 cups

Ⓓ 10 cups

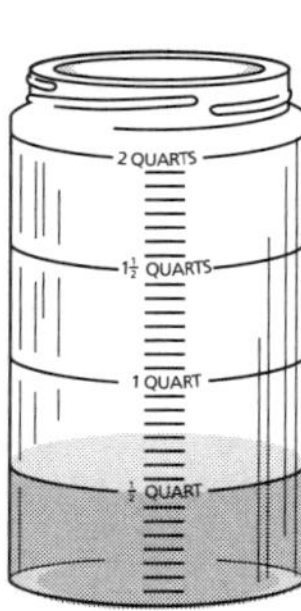

© Houghton Mifflin Harcourt Publishing Company

NAME ____

25. What is the value of the **1** in 3,**1**75?

(A) 1 (B) 10 (C) 100 (D) 1000

26. Which number shows *six thousand, one hundred four*?

(A) 6,104 (B) 6,140 (C) 6,014 (D) 6,410

27. 36¢ + 44¢ =

(A) 90¢ (B) 80¢ (C) 70¢ (D) 60¢

28. Which set of coins makes $1.00?

(A) 3 quarters, 2 dimes, 1 nickel
(B) 3 quarters, 3 dimes, 5 pennies
(C) 2 quarters, 3 dimes, 2 nickels
(D) 2 quarters, 4 dimes, 5 pennies

29. The chart shows how many times four children flipped a penny. Which child probably came closest to getting half heads and half tails?

(A) Ricardo
(B) Georgia
(C) Henry
(D) Linda

Child	Number of Flips
Ricardo	78
Georgia	104
Henry	32
Linda	56

30. At the beach, Maria found 29 clam shells, 41 scallop shells, and 62 cowrie shells. About how many shells did she find in all?

(A) 70 (B) 90 (C) 110 (D) 130

© Houghton Mifflin Harcourt Publishing Company

POST TEST

NAME ______________________________

Directions: Write your answer to each question.

1. What are the next three shapes in this pattern?

2. How many equal sides does this triangle have? __________

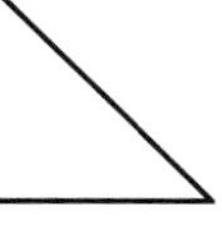

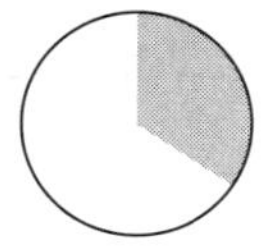

3. What fraction of this circle is shaded? __________

4. Maury had 9 pencils. He gave 5 pencils to his brother. Write a number sentence that tells how many pencils Maury has now.

____

5. Complete each number sentence. $8 \times$ ________ $= 32$

$4 \times$ ________ $= 32$

6. Divide. $54 \div 9 =$ __________

7. Write a multiplication sentence to tell how many bananas there are in all.

____

8. Add.

$$\begin{array}{r} 64 \\ +14 \\ \hline \end{array}$$

© Houghton Mifflin Harcourt Publishing Company

NAME ____

9. What is 83 rounded to the nearest ten? __________

10. Write $<$ or $>$ to make each expression true.

42 ________ 58   70 ________ 58

11. A blanket is 200 centimeters long. How many meters is that? __________

12. A bowl holds 32 ounces of water. How many cups is that? ______________

13. To measure the length of a school playground, should you use feet or yards? ______________

14. Look at the square.
What is the area of the square? ___________

15. How many minutes are in $\frac{3}{4}$ hour? __________

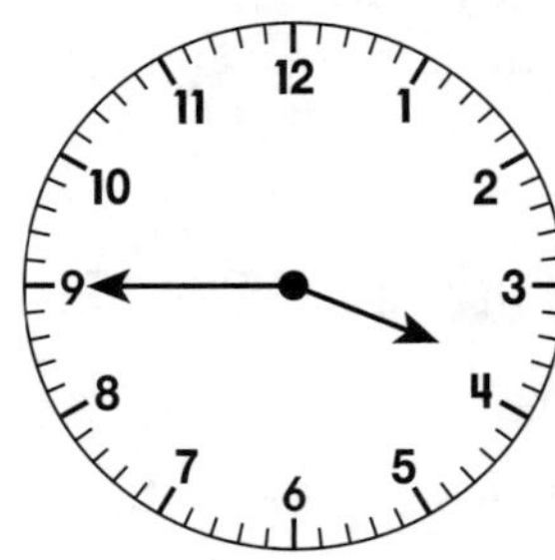

16. What time does this clock show? __________

17. What is the value of these coins? __________

18. What number is 20,000 + 4,000 + 800 + 9?

Write the number. _________________

© Houghton Mifflin Harcourt Publishing Company

NAME ______________________________

Directions: Choose the best answer to each question. Mark your answer.

19. In which group are all the numbers odd?

Ⓐ 3, 4, 5, 6
Ⓑ 3, 7, 9, 11
Ⓒ 3, 6, 9, 12
Ⓓ 3, 8, 13, 18

20. Which of these is a rectangle?

Ⓐ 
Ⓑ 
Ⓒ 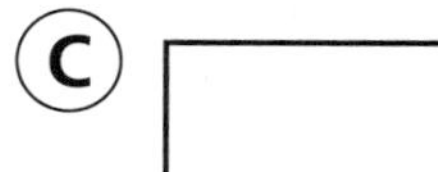
Ⓓ 

21. Which of these is a cone?

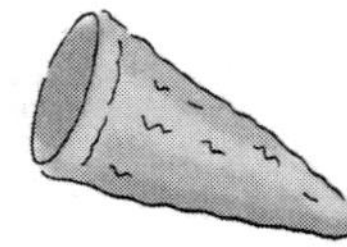
Ⓑ 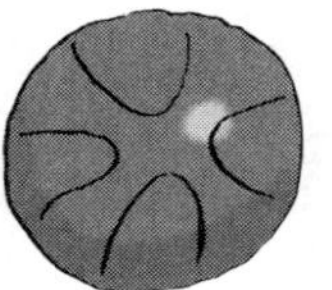
Ⓒ 

Ⓓ 

22. What number sentence goes with this Blank Hundred Chart?

Ⓐ $54 - 46 = 8$
Ⓑ $100 + 54 = 154$
Ⓒ $146 - 46 = 100$
Ⓓ $46 + 54 = 100$

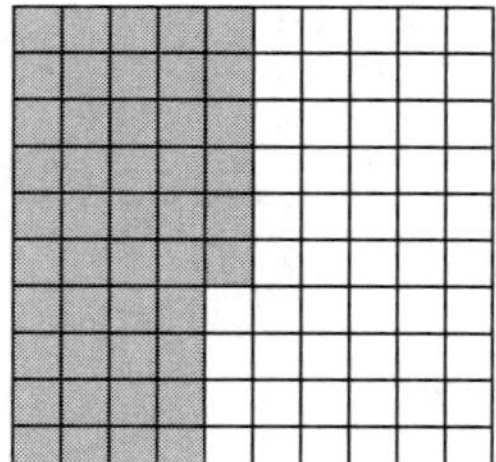

23. What is the value of the **9** in 7,**9**42?

Ⓐ 9
Ⓑ 90
Ⓒ 900
Ⓓ 9,000

24. How many fives are there in 300?

Ⓐ 60
Ⓑ 70
Ⓒ 100
Ⓓ 150

© Houghton Mifflin Harcourt Publishing Company

NAME ______________________________

25. Third graders made this graph to show which sports they like best. Which sport did the fewest students choose?

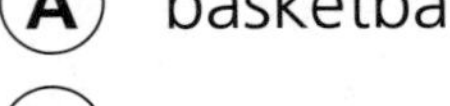

Ⓐ basketball

Ⓑ soccer

Ⓒ softball

Ⓓ football

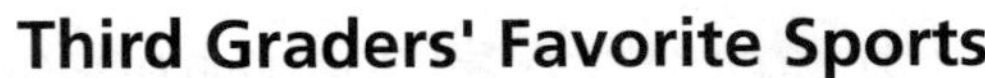

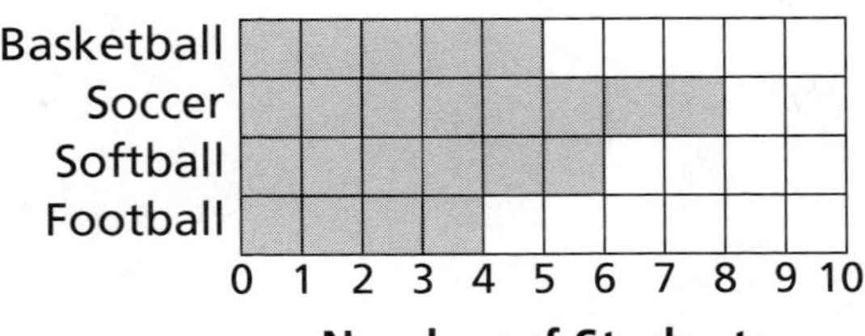

26. The chart shows how many times four friends flipped a coin. Which friend had the least chance of flipping half heads and half tails?

Ⓐ Becky

Ⓑ Ophir

Ⓒ Lenore

Ⓓ Mick

Name	Number of Flips
Becky	26
Ophir	90
Lenore	44
Mick	130

27. Nessa worked on her science project for two hours. If she finished at 1:30 P.M., when did Nessa start working?

Ⓐ 3:30 P.M. Ⓑ 11:30 P.M. Ⓒ 3:30 A.M. Ⓓ 11:30 A.M.

28. An ice cream bar costs 66¢. If Carlos pays for it with one dollar, how much change should he get back?

Ⓐ 24¢ Ⓑ 34¢ Ⓒ 44¢ Ⓓ 54¢

29. May has three dollars, five quarters, two dimes, and one penny. How much money is that?

Ⓐ $3.46 Ⓑ $3.50 Ⓒ $4.46 Ⓓ $4.50

30. Leo plays the drums for 23 minutes on Monday. He plays for 37 minutes on Tuesday and 29 minutes on Wednesday. About how many minutes does he play the drums in all?

Ⓐ 60 Ⓑ 90 Ⓒ 120 Ⓓ 150

© Houghton Mifflin Harcourt Publishing Company

NAME ______________________________

MONTHLY ASSESSMENT

Use the calendar.

What do you notice about the:

1. the even numbered calendar pieces?

____

2. the odd numbered calendar pieces?

____

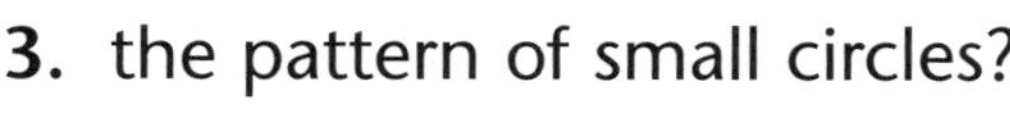

3. the pattern of small circles?

____

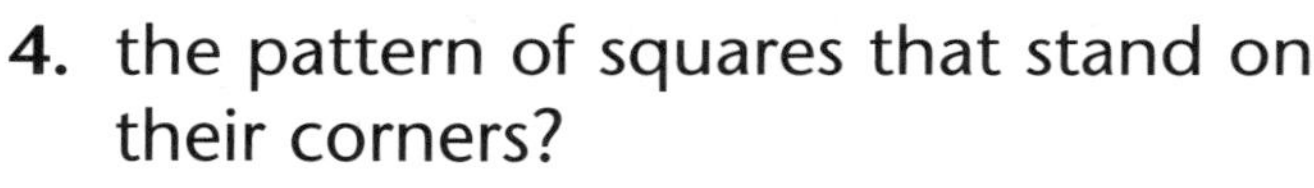

4. the pattern of squares that stand on their corners?

____

5. Count by 3s on the calendar. Which of these pieces are even numbers?

____

6. Describe the calendar pattern for this month.

____

____

Complete the patterns:

7. 3, 6, 9, _______, 15, _______, _______.

8. 4, 8, 12, 16, _______, _______, _______.

© Houghton Mifflin Harcourt Publishing Company

NAME ____________________

MONTHLY ASSESSMENT

1. List all the doubles facts from 5 + 5 to 10 + 10.

____

____

____

____

____

____

2. List all the doubles plus 1 facts from 5 + 6 to 10 + 11.

____

____

____

____

____

____

Add.

3. 11 + 12 = ______ **4.** 15 + 16 = ______ **5.** 20 + 21 = ______

6. 30 + 31 = ______ **7.** 50 + 51 = ______ **8.** 100 + 101 = ______

© Houghton Mifflin Harcourt Publishing Company

NAME ______________________________

MONTHLY ASSESSMENT

Complete the pattern on the calendar.

© Houghton Mifflin Harcourt Publishing Company

NAME ____

MONTHLY ASSESSMENT

1. There are 4 cups in a quart.
   How many cups are there in 2 quarts? _______

2. How many cups are there in 3 quarts? _______

3. How many cups are there in 4 quarts? _______

4. There are 2 cups in a pint.
   How many pints are there in 1 quart? _______

5. How many pints are there in 3 quarts? _______

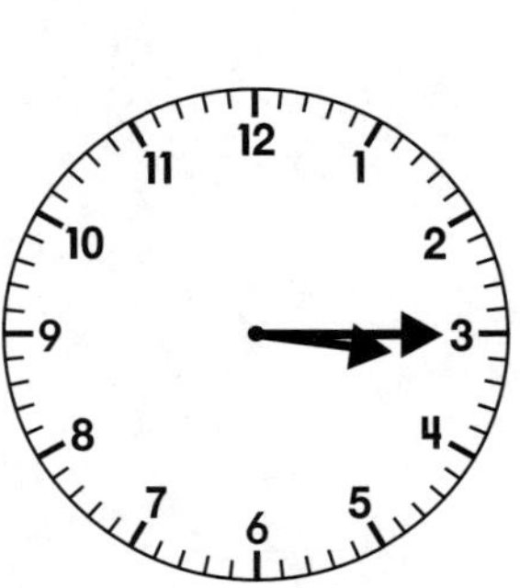

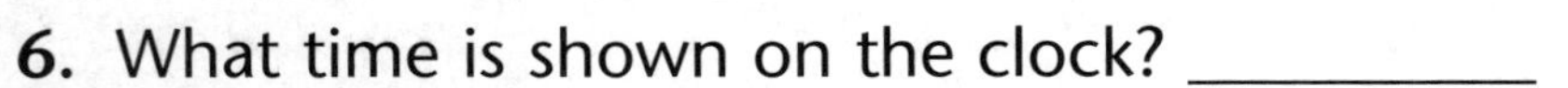

6. What time is shown on the clock? __________

7. What time will it be 15 minutes later? __________

8. What time will it be one half hour after that? __________

9. Draw hands on the clock to show that time.

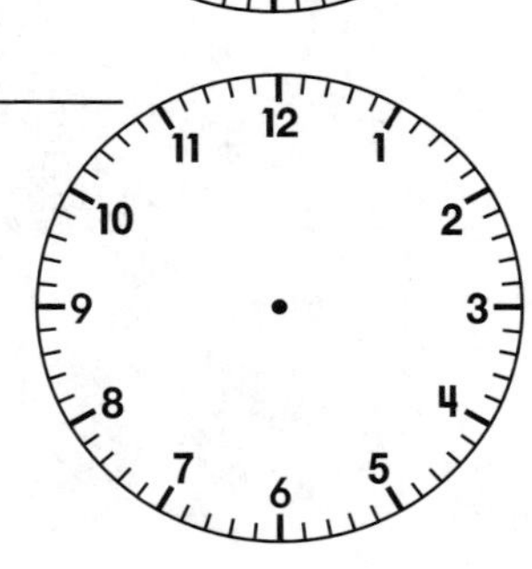

10. How much money is shown here? ______________

11. What single coin is equal in value to two dimes
    and one nickel? ______________

12. How many nickels does it take to equal the value
    of two dimes? ______________

13. How many dimes does it take to equal the value
    of two quarters? ______________

© Houghton Mifflin Harcourt Publishing Company

NAME ______________________________

MONTHLY ASSESSMENT

Use the calendar.

1. Which calendar pieces have big circles on them?

   ____

   What do you notice about this pattern?

   ____

2. Which calendar pieces have small circles on them?

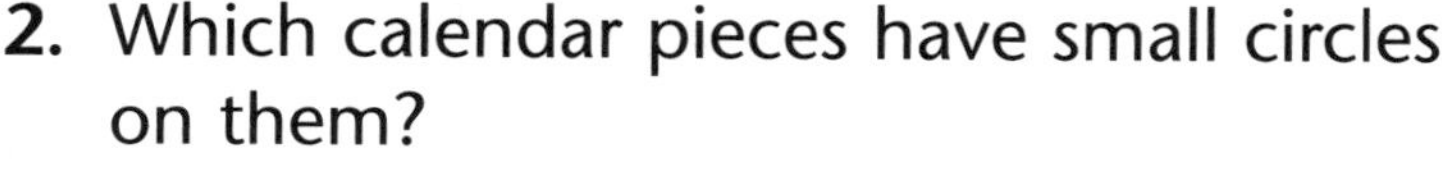

   ____

   What do you notice about this pattern?

   ____

3. What is different between the triangles on the numbers 1, 3, 6, 8 and those on 2, 4, 7, 9?

   ____

   ____

4. Complete the pattern on the calendar.

5. Suppose the first Sunday of the month is a big circle. What day of the week will be the next big circle? Why?

   ____

Continue these patterns.

6. 10, 20, 30, ______, ______, ______, 70, ______

7. 45, 40, 35, 30, ______, ______, 15, ______, ______

8. 10, 15, 25, 30, ______, ______, 55, ______, ______

© Houghton Mifflin Harcourt Publishing Company

NAME ______________________________

MONTHLY ASSESSMENT

Add.

1. $8 + 8 =$ ______ 2. $8 + 9 =$ ______ 3. $8 + 7 =$ ______

4. $6 + 5 =$ ______ 5. $7 + 6 =$ ______ 6. $9 + 10 =$ ______

Subtract.

7. $15 - 7 =$ ______ 8. $15 - 8 =$ ______ 9. $12 - 6 =$ ______

10. $17 - 9 =$ ______ 11. $18 - 9 =$ ______ 12. $13 - 7 =$ ______

Add or Subtract.

13. $8 + 10 =$ ______ 14. $36 - 10 =$ ______ 15. $36 - 20 =$ ______

16. $30 + 9 =$ ______ 17. $50 + 6 =$ ______ 18. $77 - 40 =$ ______

Fill in the missing numbers.

19. $30 -$ ______ $= 14$ 20. $31 - 16 =$ ______ 21. $44 -$ ______ $= 24$

22. ______ $- 10 = 26$ 23. $53 -$ ______ $= 33$ 24. $53 - 30 =$ ______

25. $81 -$ ______ $= 41$ 26. $50 + 8 =$ ______ 27. $40 +$ ______ $= 49$

55 85 37 60 15 67 20 95 44

28. Draw a box around the numbers you say when counting by 10's.

29. Draw a ring around the numbers you say when counting by 5's.

© Houghton Mifflin Harcourt Publishing Company

NAME ______________________________

MONTHLY ASSESSMENT

1. In Mathville, Mrs. Neville, Mr. Garcia, and Mrs. Wilson are third-grade teachers. There are 76 third-grade students in the school. Mrs. Neville's class has 26 students. Mr. Garcia's class has 25 students. How many students are there all together in these two classrooms? _______

2. How many students are in Mrs. Wilson's classroom? _______

3. Yesterday we had $465.00 in the Daily Depositor. Today we will add $31.00. How much money will we have then? _________

4. How much more money do we need to have $600.00? _________

5. There are 24 students in a class. They need to make even teams to compete in the school spelling bee. How many different ways can they make even teams? List all the possibilities.

____

____

____

Fill in the table.

	Quarters	Dimes	Nickels
6. Make 60¢ using 3 coins.			
7. Make 60¢ using 4 coins.			
8. Make 60¢ using 5 coins.			
9. Make 60¢ using 6 coins.			
10. Make 60¢ using 7 coins.			
11. Make 60¢ using 8 coins.			

© Houghton Mifflin Harcourt Publishing Company

NAME ______________________________

MONTHLY ASSESSMENT

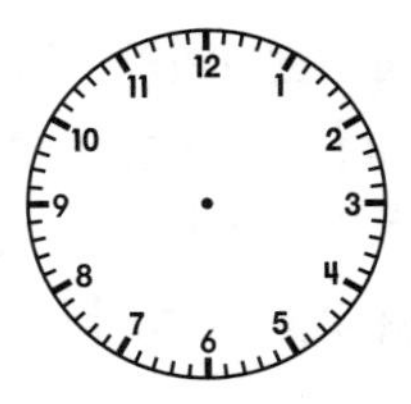
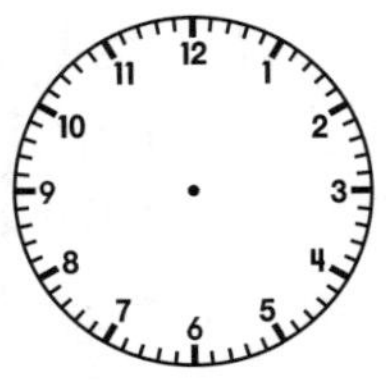

1. Draw hands on the first clock to show 8:00.

2. Draw hands on the second clock to show the time ten minutes later.

3. Draw hands on the third clock to show the time twenty minutes after that.

For each problem, decide if it is A.M. or P.M.
Draw a ring around your answer.

4. The clock shows 6:00. You are eating dinner. A.M. P.M.

5. The clock shows 10:00. You are at school. A.M. P.M.

6. The clock shows 12:00. You are eating lunch. A.M. P.M.

Draw a ring around the best answer.

7. Which unit would you use to measure the distance from one city to another?

yard mile

8. Which unit would you use to measure the weight of a dog?

ounce pound

9. Which unit would you use to measure the length of a pencil?

inch foot

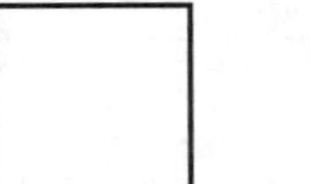

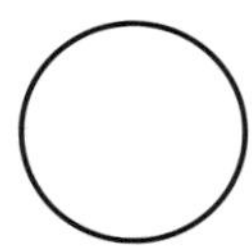

10. Draw a box around the triangle.

11. Draw a ring around the square.

© Houghton Mifflin Harcourt Publishing Company

NAME ______________________________

MONTHLY ASSESSMENT

Use the calendar.

1. What do you notice about the pieces that have circles on them?

   ____

2. What is an even number?

   ____

3. Describe the calendar pattern this month.

   ____

   ____

4. Complete the pattern on the calendar.

5. Which rhombuses have circles on them? Why? ______________________________

   ____

6. How are the square and rhombus different? ______________________________

   ____

7. How are the rectangle on the 1st and the rectangle on the 4th different?

   ____

Complete the patterns.

8. 5, 11, 17, 23, _______, _______, _______.

9. 3, 9, 15, _______, _______, _______

© Houghton Mifflin Harcourt Publishing Company

NAME ______________________________

MONTHLY ASSESSMENT

1. Write and solve three problems that add nine to a number.

+ ______ + ______ + ______

2. Explain how you solved these problems.

____

____

3. Write and solve three problems that subtract nine from a number.

− ______ − ______ − ______

4. Explain how you solved these problems.

____

____

Add or Subtract.

5. $39 + 6$

6. $36 - 16$

7. $299 + 7$

8. $179 + 8$

9. $45 - 25$

10. $64 - 40$

© Houghton Mifflin Harcourt Publishing Company

NAME ____________________

MONTHLY ASSESSMENT

The students in Mathville sold pencils, rulers, pens, and markers to raise money for their school. The table shows how many of each item they sold for two days. Use the table to answer the questions.

	Friday	Saturday
pencils	20	48
rulers	2	10
pens	19	33
markers	9	26

1. How many pencils did they sell all together? _______
2. How many more markers did they sell on Saturday than on Friday? _______
3. How many pens did they sell all together? _______
4. Which item did they sell the fewest of? _______________
5. Which item did they sell the most of? _______________
6. How many markers did they sell all together? _______
7. On which day did they sell more items? _______________
8. Kiesha keeps all her marbles in a box. She has 10 blue marbles, 5 red marbles, 7 green marbles, and 3 yellow marbles. How many marbles does she have all together? _______
9. If she reaches into the box and pulls out one marble without looking, what color marble is she most likely to pull out? _______________
10. Explain your thinking. ____

____

© Houghton Mifflin Harcourt Publishing Company

NAME ______________________________

MONTHLY ASSESSMENT

1. Name three things in your classroom that you think are about one foot long.

____

2. Name three things in your classroom that you think are about one yard long.

____

3. Name three things in your house that you think are about one yard long.

____

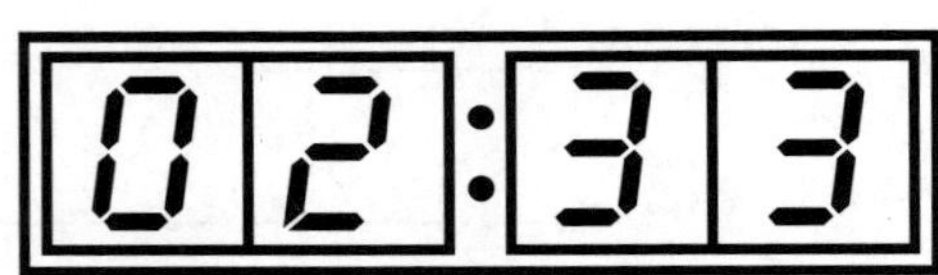

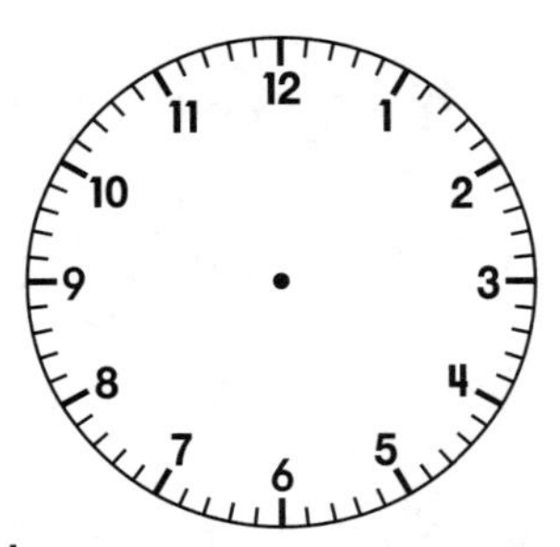

4. Draw hands on the clock showing the same time displayed on the digital clock.

5. What time will it be 30 minutes later? __________

6. There are three feet in one yard. How many feet are there in three yards? _______

7. How many feet are there in five yards? _______

8. There are twelve inches in one foot. How many inches are there in two feet? _______

9. How many inches are there in $\frac{1}{2}$ foot? _______

© Houghton Mifflin Harcourt Publishing Company

NAME ______________________________

MONTHLY ASSESSMENT

Use the calendar.

1. Describe the pattern for this month?

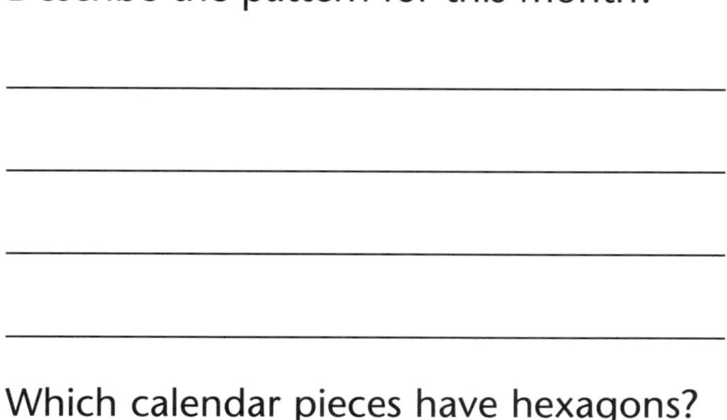

2. Which calendar pieces have hexagons?

____

3. Which hexagons have stars?

____

4. How can the first trapezoid be made into the second trapezoid?

____

5. If the area of the hexagon is 1 square unit, what is the area of the trapezoid?

____

6. How many halves make 2 wholes? _______

Complete the patterns:

7. 6, 12, 18, 24, _______, _______, _______

8. 1, 2, 4, 5, 7, 8, 10, 11, _______, _______, _______

9. 27, 21, 15, _______, _______, _______

© Houghton Mifflin Harcourt Publishing Company

NAME ______________________________

MONTHLY ASSESSMENT

Add or Subtract.

1. 7 + 5 = ______
2. 14 − 8 = ______
3. 19 − 10 = ______
4. 4 + 9 = ______
5. 16 − 9 = ______
6. 17 − 9 = ______
7. 18 − 9 = ______
8. 13 − 7 = ______
9. 8 + 7 = ______

Add.

10. 56 + 56
11. 143 + 47
12. 300 + 437
13. 250 + 101
14. 77 + 73
15. 311 + 199
16. 634 + 512
17. 19 + 321
18. 210 + 456

Subtract.

19. 80 − 23
20. 465 − 256
21. 712 − 310
22. 173 − 85
23. 840 − 326
24. 35 − 17
25. 505 − 26
26. 47 − 19
27. 621 − 223

© Houghton Mifflin Harcourt Publishing Company

NAME ______________________________

MONTHLY ASSESSMENT

Use the digits 2, 3, 4, 5, and 6 to make the sums side to side (horizontally) and up and down (vertically).

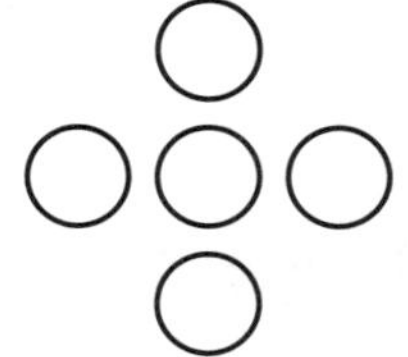

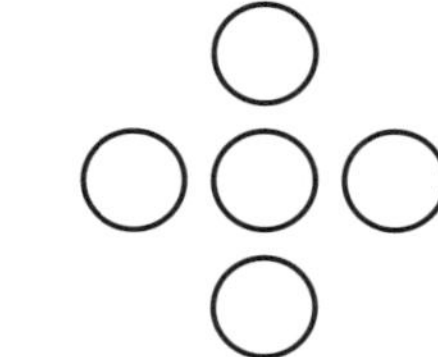

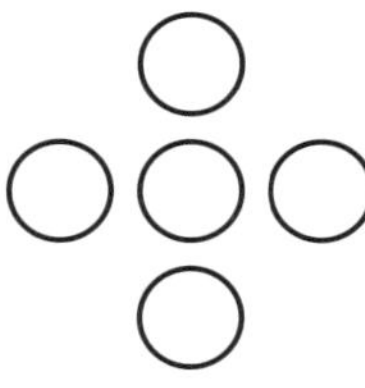

1. Make the sum 11.
2. What number is in the middle circle?

   ____

3. Make the sum 12.
4. What number is in the middle circle?

   ____

5. Make the sum 13.
6. What number is in the middle circle?

   ____

7. What is the pattern of the numbers in the middle circle? ____________

   ____

Try using the digits 3, 4, 5, 6, and 7.

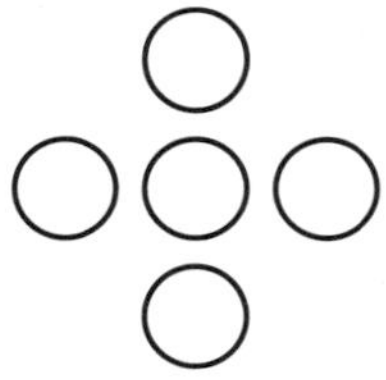

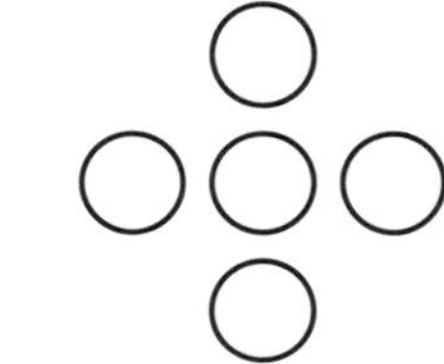

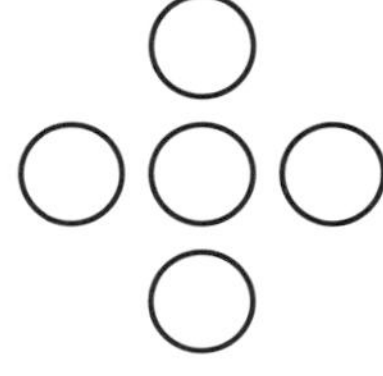

8. Make the sum 14.
9. What number is in the middle circle?

   ____

10. Make the sum 15.
11. What number is in the middle circle?

   ____

12. Make the sum 16.
13. What number is in the middle circle?

   ____

14. Write two addition sentences and two subtraction sentences that equal the number of the new year.

   ____

   ____

© Houghton Mifflin Harcourt Publishing Company

NAME ______________________________

MONTHLY ASSESSMENT

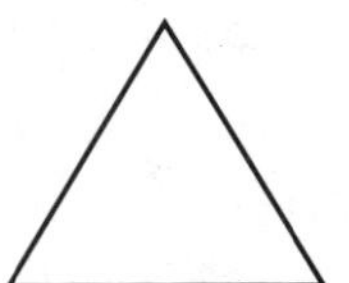 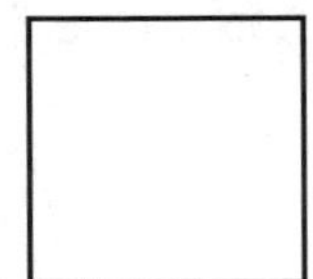 

1. If each side of the triangle is one inch long, how many inches long are the sides of the triangle all together? _______

2. If each side of the square is two inches long, how many inches long are the sides of the square all together? _______

3. How many sides does the star have? _______

4. If each side of the star is one inch long, how many inches long are the sides of the star all together? _______

5. Rosa went to the store and bought an eraser for 71¢. She paid with a one-dollar bill. How much change did she get back?

   ____

6. What is the least number of coins you could use to make that amount? _______

7. What coins are they? ______________________________

8. Write another way to make that amount.

   ____

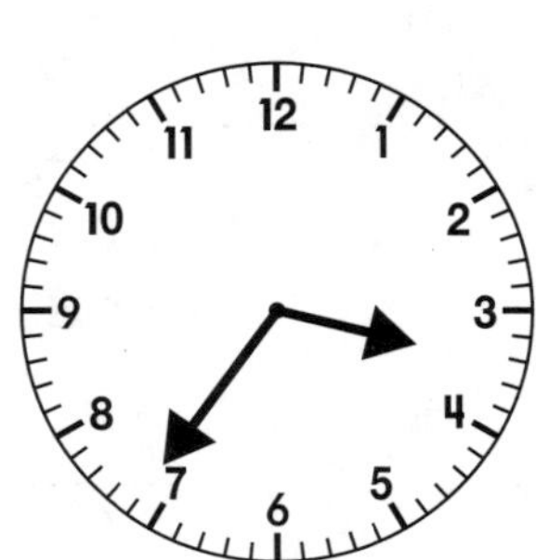

9. How many minutes past the hour is it? _______

10. What hour is it? _______________

11. What time is it? _______________

12. How many minutes until the next hour? _______

13. What time will it be then? _______________

© Houghton Mifflin Harcourt Publishing Company

NAME ____________________

MONTHLY ASSESSMENT

Use the calendar.

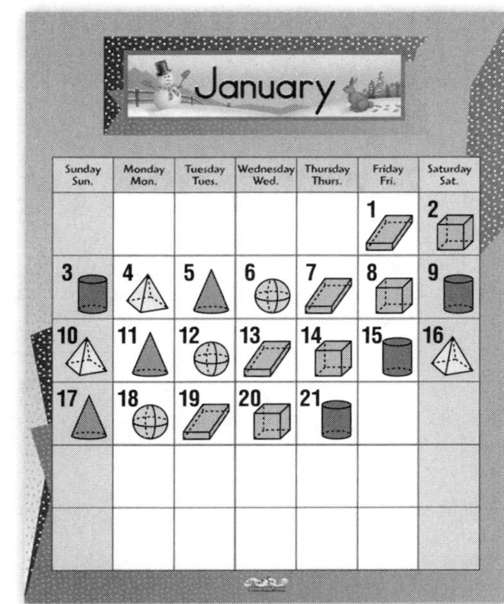

1. Describe the pattern this month.

____

____

2. How many days does it take to make a complete pattern? _______

3. January has 31 days. How many complete patterns will there be in January?

____

4. How many more days will be left? _______

What do you notice about the pieces that have:

5. spheres on them? ____________________

7. cylinders on them? ____________________

Circle the correct letter.

8. Cubes have:

   a. curved edges. **b.** 6 square faces. **c.** no square faces.

9. Cylinders have:

   a. 4 circle bases. **b.** a curved surface. **c.** 2 corners.

10. Why are the spheres arranged diagonally to the left on the calendar?

____

____

© Houghton Mifflin Harcourt Publishing Company

NAME ______________________________

MONTHLY ASSESSMENT

1. What is the sum of 1, 2, 3, 4, and 5? _______

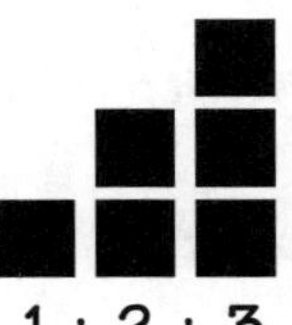

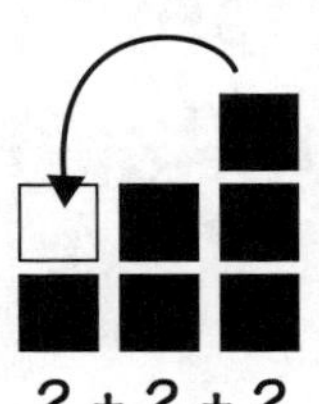

2. What is a fast way of adding these numbers?

____

____

3. What is the sum of 11, 12, and 13? _______

4. What is a fast way of adding these numbers? ______________________________

____

5. What is the sum of 13, 14, 15, 16, and 17? _______

6. What is a fast way of adding these numbers? ______________________________

____

7. What is the sum of all the numbers from 1 to 10? _______

8. Tell how you got your answer. ______________________________

____

____

Multiply.

9. $2 \times 8 =$ _______ 10. $3 \times 8 =$ _______

11. $7 \times 2 =$ _______ 12. $7 \times 3 =$ _______

13. $3 \times 5 =$ _______ 14. $2 \times 5 =$ _______

© Houghton Mifflin Harcourt Publishing Company

NAME ______________________________

MONTHLY ASSESSMENT

I'm a Number. . .

Look at the Counting Tape to answer these riddles.

1. I'm an even number between 20 and 40. Both my digits are the same. Who am I? _______
2. I'm the smallest number that rounds to 40 when you round me to the nearest 10. Who am I? _______
3. I'm an odd number between 30 and 40. The sum of my digits is 12. Who am I? _______
4. I'm a number between 20 and 29 that you say when you count by 2's and when you count by 3's. Who am I? _______
5. I'm the number you get when you round 32 to the nearest ten. Who am I? _______

Solve these problems.

6. In a school survey about favorite colors, 39 students liked red and 56 liked blue. How many more students liked blue than red? _______
7. In a third-grade classroom at another school, there are twice as many girls as boys. There are 7 boys in the class. How many students are in the class all together? _______
8. How did you get your answer? ______________________________

____

© Houghton Mifflin Harcourt Publishing Company

NAME ______________________________

MONTHLY ASSESSMENT

1. What time does the clock show? __________

2. What time will it be in 10 minutes? __________

3. What time was it 20 minutes ago? __________

4. How many minutes until the next hour? ______

5. What time will it be then? __________

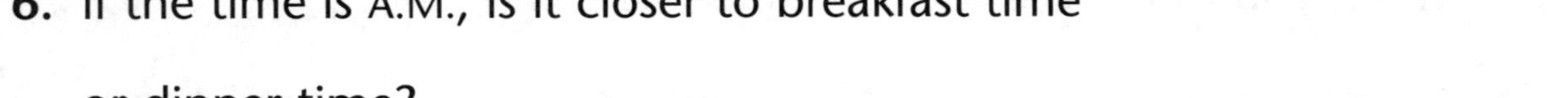

6. If the time is A.M., is it closer to breakfast time

   or dinner time? ______________________________

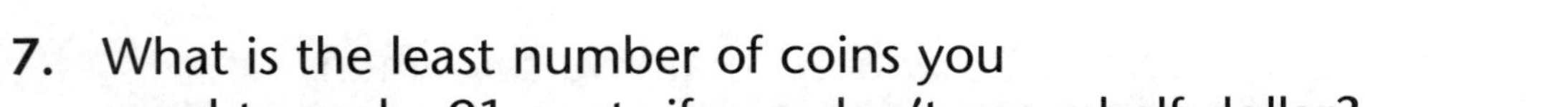

7. What is the least number of coins you need to make 91 cents if you don't use a half-dollar? ______

8. What coins did you use? ______________________________

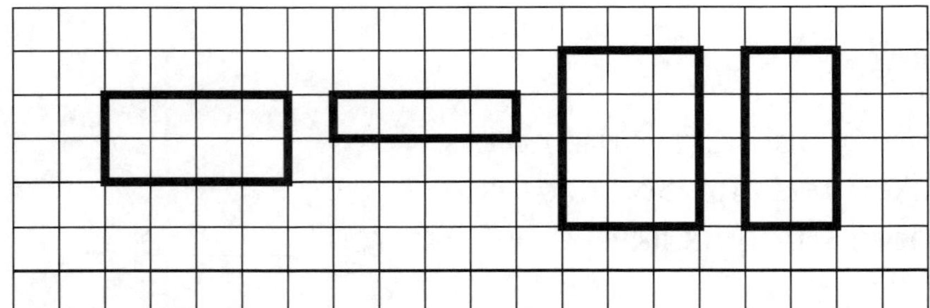

9. Draw a ring around the two rectangles that are the same size and shape.

10. How many sides are there on two rectangles? ______

11. How many sides are there on four rectangles? ______

12. How many sides are there on eight rectangles? ______

© Houghton Mifflin Harcourt Publishing Company

NAME ______________________________

MONTHLY ASSESSMENT

Use the calendar.

1. What fraction follows this pattern on the calendar? 2, 6, 10, 14, 18? _____

2. What is the number pattern for the pieces with $\frac{1}{3}$ of the circle shaded?

   ____

   What fraction of a $\frac{1}{3}$ circle is not shaded?

   ____

3. How many days does it take to make a complete pattern? _______

4. February has 28 days. How many times will the pattern repeat? ______

5. Will the pieces that are one whole ever repeat more than 7 times?

   When? ______________________________

6. Which is larger, $\frac{1}{3}$ or $\frac{1}{4}$? Why? ______________________________

   ____

7. Suppose the pattern continued on.
   What fraction will be on the next Friday? _______

8. Suppose the pattern continued on.
   Which pieces would have the next three $\frac{1}{4}$ on them? _____________

9. Why are the $\frac{1}{4}$ pieces arranged diagonally to the right on the calendar?

   ____

   ____

© Houghton Mifflin Harcourt Publishing Company

NAME ______________________________

MONTHLY ASSESSMENT

1. Describe a fast way of adding 99, 100, and 101. ____________

____

____

2. What is the sum? ________

3. What is the sum of 97, 98, 99, 100, 101, and 102? ________

4. Describe how you got your answer. ____________

____

What Number Am I?

5. I am the number of quarters in ten dollars. What number am I? ______

6. I am the number of legs on six chairs. What number am I? _______

7. I am the number of cups in two quarts. What number am I? _______

8. I am the number of quarts in five gallons. What number am I? _______

9. I am the number of tires on eight cars. What number am I? _______

10. I am the number of cups in one gallon. What number am I? _______

11. I am the number of legs on seven cats. What number am I? _______

12. I am the number of sides on nine squares. What number am I? ______

13. I am the number of feet in four yards. What number am I? _______

Subtract. Try to do these mentally.

14. $\begin{array}{r} 5764 \\ -101 \\ \hline \end{array}$

15. $\begin{array}{r} 5764 \\ -199 \\ \hline \end{array}$

16. $\begin{array}{r} 3205 \\ -99 \\ \hline \end{array}$

17. $\begin{array}{r} 3205 \\ -299 \\ \hline \end{array}$

© Houghton Mifflin Harcourt Publishing Company

NAME ______________________________

MONTHLY ASSESSMENT

Use the Hundreds Chart to help you.

1	2	3	4	5	6	7	8	9	10
11	12	13	14	15	16	17	18	19	20
21	22	23	24	25	26	27	28	29	30
31	32	33	34	35	36	37	38	39	40
41	42	43	44	45	46	47	48	49	50
51	52	53	54	55	56	57	58	59	60
61	62	63	64	65	66	67	68	69	70
71	72	73	74	75	76	77	78	79	80
81	82	83	84	85	86	87	88	89	90
91	92	93	94	95	96	97	98	99	100

1. When rounding to the nearest ten, what is the largest number that rounds to 90? ______
2. When rounding to the nearest ten, what is the smallest number that rounds to 90? ______
3. When rounding to the nearest ten, what number will 96 round to? ______
4. Explain your thinking. ______________________________

   ____
5. What number is exactly halfway between 90 and 100? ______
6. Look at the numbers between 80 and 100. When rounding to the nearest ten, do more of these numbers round up or down? ______
7. Explain your thinking. ______________________________

   ____

Think of the numbers you say when you count by 5's. Then think of the numbers you say when you count by 10's.

8. What is the first number you say when counting by both 5's and 10's? ______
9. When you count by both 5's and 10's, are the numbers you say even or odd numbers? __________
10. How do you know? ______________________________

    ____

© Houghton Mifflin Harcourt Publishing Company

NAME ______________________________

MONTHLY ASSESSMENT

1. Imagine you have a stack of 100 pennies. How many centimeters high do you estimate the stack would be? _______

2. Stack ten pennies, measure the stack, and calculate how many centimeters high a stack of 100 pennies would be. Write your answer and explain how you figured it out.

____

____

3. Compare your answer to problems 1 and 2.

   Was your estimate close? _______

4. How many sides are there on this star? _______

5. How many sides are there on two stars? _______

Try this.

6. How many sides are there on five stars? _______

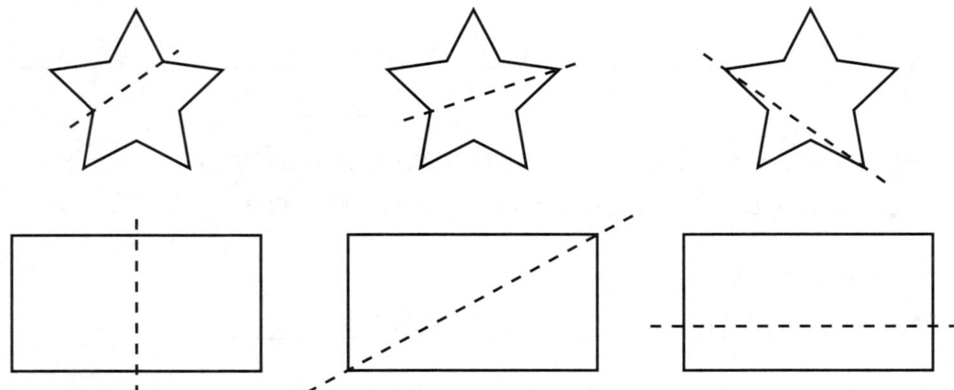

Only one of these stars and one of these rectangles show true lines of symmetry.

7. Draw a ring around the star that shows a true line of symmetry.

8. Draw a ring around the rectangle that shows a true line of symmetry.

© Houghton Mifflin Harcourt Publishing Company

NAME ______________________________

MONTHLY ASSESSMENT

1. Draw figure 5 in this pattern and fill in the blank below it.

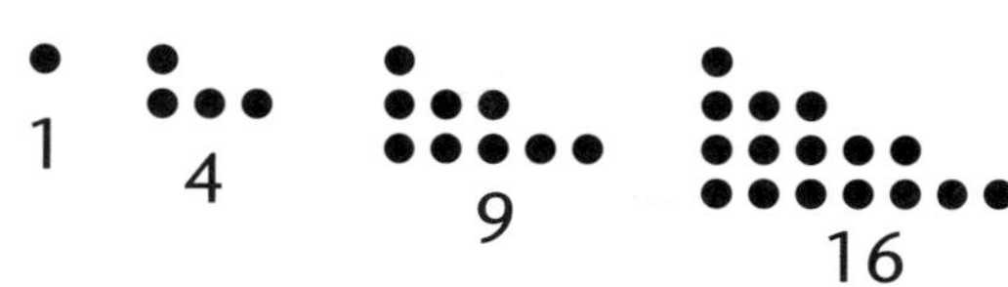

2. Draw figure 6 in the pattern and fill in the blank below it.

3. Figure 1 has how many dots? _______

4. Figure 2 has how many dots? _______

5. Figure 3 has how many dots? _______

6. Figure 4 has how many dots? _______

7. What is the relationship between each figure number and how many dots are in the figure? ______________________

____

____

____

8. How many dots will be in figure 7? _______

9. How many dots are added to figure 1 to make figure 2? _______

10. How many dots are added to figure 2 to make figure 3? _______

11. How many dots are added to figure 3 to make figure 4? _______

12. How many dots are added to figure 4 to make figure 5? _______

13. What do you notice about the number of dots that are added each time? ______________________

14. How many dots will be added to figure 6 to make figure 7? _______

© Houghton Mifflin Harcourt Publishing Company

NAME ______________________________

MONTHLY ASSESSMENT

Draw an "X" on all the numbers you say when you count by fives.

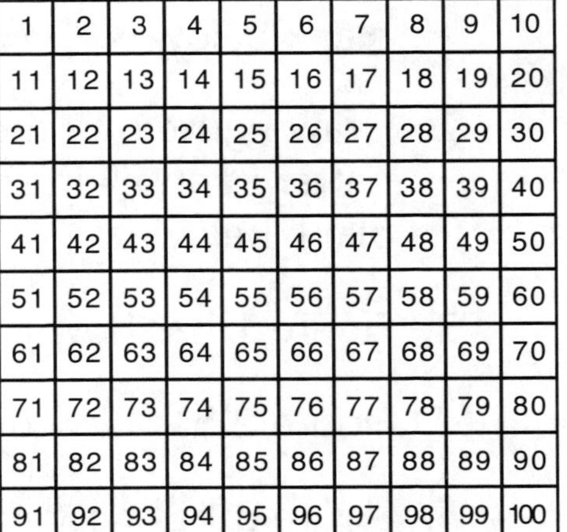

1	2	3	4	5	6	7	8	9	10
11	12	13	14	15	16	17	18	19	20
21	22	23	24	25	26	27	28	29	30
31	32	33	34	35	36	37	38	39	40
41	42	43	44	45	46	47	48	49	50
51	52	53	54	55	56	57	58	59	60
61	62	63	64	65	66	67	68	69	70
71	72	73	74	75	76	77	78	79	80
81	82	83	84	85	86	87	88	89	90
91	92	93	94	95	96	97	98	99	100

1. What do you notice about these numbers? ______________________________

____

Draw a ring on all the numbers you say when you count by tens.

2. What do you notice about these numbers?

____

____

3. What is the first number you say when you count by threes and tens? _______

4. What is the first number you say when you count by fours and tens? _______

5. What is the first number you say when you count by threes, fours, and tens? _______

Multiply.

6. $7 \times 5 =$ _______
7. $6 \times 10 =$ _______
8. $9 \times 10 =$ _______
9. $5 \times 4 =$ _______
10. $3 \times 5 =$ _______
11. $10 \times 10 =$ _______
12. $6 \times 5 =$ _______
13. $7 \times 10 =$ _______
14. $8 \times 5 =$ _______
15. $5 \times 5 =$ _______
16. $10 \times 3 =$ _______
17. $10 \times 5 =$ _______
18. $9 \times 5 =$ _______
19. $8 \times 10 =$ _______
20. $4 \times 10 =$ _______

© Houghton Mifflin Harcourt Publishing Company

NAME ____

MONTHLY ASSESSMENT

1. There are 24 students in the class. One fourth of them have blond hair. One half of them have brown hair. The rest have black hair. How many students have blond hair? ______

2. How many students have brown hair? ______

3. How many students have black hair? ______

4. How did you get your answers? ______________________

____

____

5. In the same class, one third of the students are girls. How many boys are in the class? ______

6. Describe how you got your answer, ______________________

____

Round these numbers to the nearest hundred.

7. 6213 rounds to ________ 8. 6166 rounds to ________

9. What do you notice about your answers? ______________

10. What is the smallest number that rounds to 7200 when rounded to the nearest hundred? ________

11. What is the largest number that rounds to 7400 when rounded to the nearest hundred? ________

12. A number rounds to 7100 when rounded to the nearest hundred. What could the number be? ________

13. A number rounds to 7000 when rounded to the to he nearest hundred. It is greater than 7020. What number could it be? ________

© Houghton Mifflin Harcourt Publishing Company

NAME ______________________________

MONTHLY ASSESSMENT

1. Show one half on each of these figures. You can draw a line or color part of each figure with your pencil.

2. Draw a ring around one half of these circles.

3. Draw a ring around one half of these squares.

4. Draw a ring around one fourth of theses circles.

5. Draw a ring around one fourth of these squares.

Solve these coin puzzles. Don't use half-dollars.

6. Fred has five coins worth 80 cents. What coins does he have?

____

7. Amy wants to make $1.16 (116 cents) three different ways. How can she do it using 7 coins? ______________________________

8. How can she do it using 10 coins? ______________________________

____

9. How can she do it using 13 coins? ______________________________

____

© Houghton Mifflin Harcourt Publishing Company

NAME ____

MONTHLY ASSESSMENT

Use the calendar for problems 1–8

1. Describe the pattern on the calendar.

   ____

   ____

2. How are a trapezoid and a rectangle alike? How are they different?

   ____

   ____

   ____

   ____

3. How many lines of symmetry does a rectangle have? ________

4. Draw the lines of symmetry for this square.

Look at the first six pieces on the calendar.

5. Write a fraction for the number of these pieces that have squares on them. ________________

6. Write a fraction for the number of these pieces that do not have squares on them. ________________

7. Write a division sentence to show how many times this pattern will repeat during the month.

   ________ ÷ ________ = ________

8. Suppose this pattern continued on. Which pieces would have the next three hearts on them? ____________________

© Houghton Mifflin Harcourt Publishing Company

NAME ______________________________

MONTHLY ASSESSMENT

Number sentences for the 30th day of April.
Write three number sentences that equal 30. Use only addition.

1. ______ + ______ = 30 **2.** ______ + ______ = 30

3. ______ + ______ = 30

Write three number sentences that equal 30 using only subtraction.

4. ______ − ______ = 30 **5.** ______ − ______ = 30

6. ______ − ______ = 30

Write three number sentences that equal 30 using only multiplication.

7. ______ × ______ = 30 **8.** ______ × ______ = 30

9. ______ × ______ = 30

Write three number sentences that equal 30 using multiplication and then addition. For example, 1 × 2 + 28 = 30.

10. ______ × ______ + ______ = 30

11. ______ × ______ + ______ = 30

12. ______ × ______ + ______ = 30

Divide. If there is no remainder, write a zero after the R.

13. 25 ÷ 5 = ______ R ______ **14.** 26 ÷ 5 = ______ R ______

15. 13 ÷ 6 = ______ R ______ **16.** 18 ÷ 6 = ______ R ______

17. 18 ÷ 4 = ______ R ______ **18.** 19 ÷ 2 = ______ R ______

19. 20 ÷ 4 = ______ R ______ **20.** 20 ÷ 3 = ______ R ______

© Houghton Mifflin Harcourt Publishing Company

NAME ________________________________

MONTHLY ASSESSMENT

1. Lin has 21 toothpicks. She makes some triangles and some squares with the toothpicks. How many of each shape can she make if she uses all 21 toothpicks?

   ____

2. Danny has 30 toothpicks. How many triangles can he make using all 30 toothpicks? ______

3. Will he have any toothpicks left over? If so, how many? ______

4. If Danny makes only squares, how many can he make? ______

5. Will he have any toothpicks left over? If so, how many? __________

6. Draw rings around the two rectangles that are divided into four equal parts.

  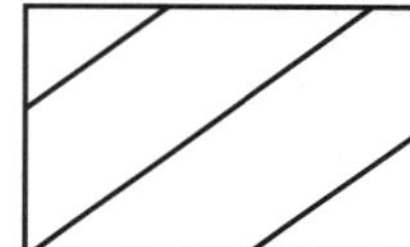 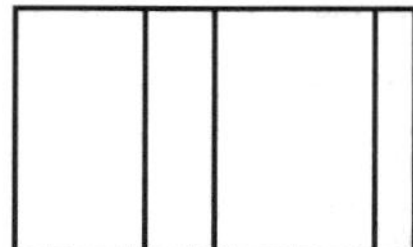

7. At the store, large stickers cost $0.25 each, medium stickers cost $0.15 each, and small stickers cost $0.06 each. How much money will you spend if you buy 3 large stickers, 5 medium stickers, and 10 small stickers?

   ____

8. If you pay for your stickers with a five-dollar bill, how much change will you get back?

   ____

© Houghton Mifflin Harcourt Publishing Company

NAME ____________________

MONTHLY ASSESSMENT

1. How many minutes are in $\frac{1}{2}$ hour? ______
2. How many minutes are in $1\frac{1}{2}$ hours? ______
3. How many minutes are in $\frac{1}{4}$ hour? ______
4. How many minutes are in $1\frac{3}{4}$ hours? ______
5. What time is shown on the clock? ________
6. What time will it be 4 hours from that time? ________

7. What time was it 1 hour earlier than that time? ________

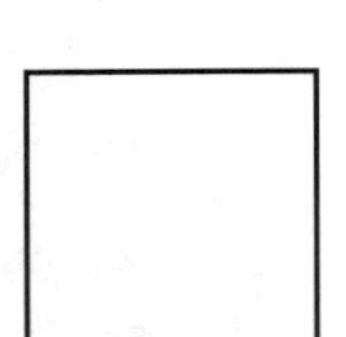

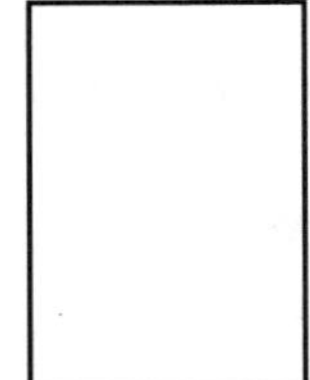

8. Write the name of each shape inside the figure.
9. Which one of these shapes has no parallel sides? __________
10. Draw rings around the shapes that have two pairs of parallel opposite sides.
11. Which figure has four equal sides? __________
12. Which two shapes have square corners? ____________________
13. How many ounces are in $\frac{1}{2}$ pound?______
14. How many ounces are in $2\frac{1}{2}$ pounds? ______
15. How many ounces are in $\frac{1}{4}$ pound? ______
16. How many ounces are in $1\frac{3}{4}$ pounds? ______

© Houghton Mifflin Harcourt Publishing Company

NAME ____

MONTHLY ASSESSMENT

Use the calendar.

1. What are the shapes on the calendar? How are they alike?

____

____

2. Describe this pattern using letters.

____

4. Write a division sentence to show how many times this pattern will repeat during the month. Is there a remainder?

_______ ÷ _______ = _______

5. Suppose this pattern continued on. What shape would be on 38? Why?

____

What shape am I?

6. I have two parallel bases and a curved surface connecting them.

a. sphere **b.** cone **c.** cylinder

7. I have one circle base and a curved surface.

a. sphere **b.** cone **c.** cylinder

8. What is another real world example of each shape on the calendar?

Cone	Cylinder	Sphere
____________	____________	____________

© Houghton Mifflin Harcourt Publishing Company

NAME ______________________________

MONTHLY ASSESSMENT

Add. Try to solve these problems mentally.

1. 205 + 85 = ______
2. 945 + 70 = ______
3. 680 + 95 = ______
4. 475 + 76 = ______

Fill in the blanks to make the quantities represented on both sides of the equal sign the same.

5. 40 ÷ 10 = 20 ÷ ______
6. 8 × 8 = 16 × ______
7. 75 − 50 = 99 − ______
8. 15 ÷ 3 = 30 ÷ ______
9. 7 × 6 = ______ × 3
10. 120 − 95 = ______ − 120

Fill in the blank after each numbered problem with the letter of the correct solution. Try to solve these problems mentally.

11. 38 + 47 = ______ A. 248
12. 150 − 28 = ______ B. 85
13. 1000 − 752 = ______ C. 122
14. 855 − 245 = ______ D. 301
15. 150 + 151 = ______ E. 610

Arrange the numbers below each set of empty boxes inside the grid so that the number in the middle box is the result of multiplying the numbers to its right and left and also the result of multiplying the numbers above and below it. In each problem, there is one number that doesn't belong. Draw a ring around it.

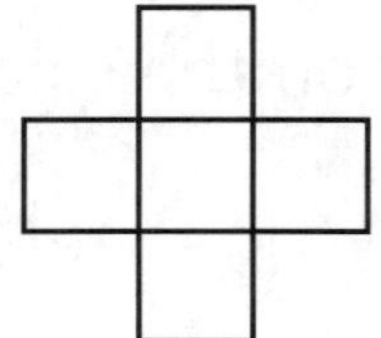
16. 2, 3, 4, 6, 8, 12

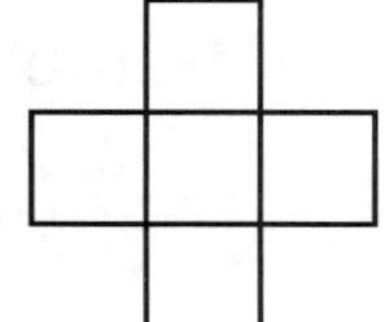
17. 3, 5, 6, 10, 30, 35

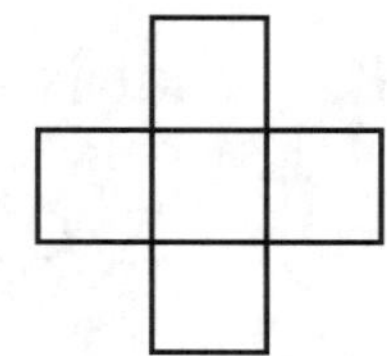
18. 2, 4, 6, 12, 24, 28

© Houghton Mifflin Harcourt Publishing Company

NAME ______________________________

MONTHLY ASSESSMENT

1. A rainbow displays colors in the order red, orange, yellow, green, blue, indigo, and violet. How many colors are displayed in 2 rainbows? _______

2. How many colors are displayed in 4 rainbows? _______

3. How many colors are displayed in 8 rainbows? _______

Write stories for each of these division sentences.

4. $25 \div 5 = 5$ ______________________________

____

5. $15 \div 4 = 3$ R3 ______________________________

____

For each of these problems, first tell whether you would use addition, subtraction, multiplication, or division to solve it. Then solve each problem.

6. Rita, Samantha, and Margarita each bought a bag of marbles at the store. Each bag had 10 marbles in it. How many marbles did they have all together? _______________

7. Kathy opened a carton of 12 eggs to make a cake. She discovered that 5 of the eggs were broken. How many unbroken eggs were left in the carton? _______________

8. Three friends were counting blue cars on different streets in their town. Tom saw 14. Miguel saw 9. Lee saw 8. How many cars did they count all together? _______________

9. Richard has ten pieces of gum to share with four of his friends. How many pieces of gum will each friend get? _______________

© Houghton Mifflin Harcourt Publishing Company

NAME ______________________________

MONTHLY ASSESSMENT

Who Am I?

1. I am a solid figure with five faces. Four of my faces are the same and one is different. I have five corners. Who am I? ______________

2. I am a solid figure with no flat faces. If you put me on the floor and tap me, I will roll. Who am I? ______________

3. I am a solid figure with only one flat face and a curved surface. Who am I? ______________

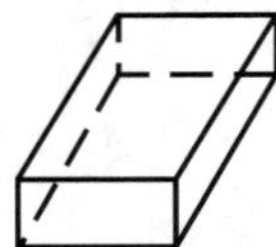

4. I am a solid figure with eight square corners and six faces. My faces are not all the same size. Who am I? ______________

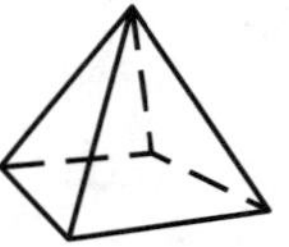

Draw a ring around the best answer.

5. What unit would you use to measure how much water is in a full fish tank?

   cup quart

6. What unit would you use to measure the width of your little finger?

   centimeter meter

7. What unit would you use to measure the distance from your knee to the floor?

   foot yard

8. What unit would you use to measure the weight of a small stone?

   ounce pound

9. What unit would you use to measure how much soda all the students in your school might drink in one week?

   milliliter liter

© Houghton Mifflin Harcourt Publishing Company

Assessment Checklist

Child ______________________ **Age** ________

Observation Dates ______ ______ ______ ______ ______ ______ ______

Circle or check the appropriate item below when a child shows understanding. Use different-colored ink each time you observe so the items and the dates will correspond. Space is provided for additional notes.

Number Sense		**Notes**
N1 counts beyond 1,000: by ones, by tens, by hundreds	☐	______
N2 compares and orders quantities to 9,999	☐	______
N3 writes comparison sentences	☐	______
N4 understands place value to thousands	☐	______
N5 counts mixed coins	☐	______
N6 trades and regroups: pennies, dimes, ones, tens, hundreds	☐	______
N7 decomposes and recombines numbers	☐	______
N8 identifies multiples of 10	☐	______
N9 rounds to the nearest ten	☐	______
N10 reads and writes decimal amounts	☐	______
N11 understands fractions: as parts of a whole, as parts of a set	☐	______
N12 shows developing number sense	☐	______

Computation		
C1 knows basic addition and subtraction facts to 18	☐	______
C2 regroups to: add, subtract	☐	______
C3 adds and subtracts: two-digit numbers, three-digit numbers	☐	______
C4 adds and subtracts: like fractions, unlike fractions	☐	______

© Houghton Mifflin Harcourt Publishing Company

ASSESSMENT CHECKLIST continued

CHILD ______________________________

Computation (continued)

Notes

			Notes
C5	understands ounces as fractional parts of pounds	☐	
C6	adds and subtracts mentally	☐	
C7	computes using money amounts	☐	
C8	uses a variety of strategies to add and subtract	☐	
C9	understands the concept of equal groups	☐	
C10	sees multiplication as repeated addition	☐	
C11	visualizes multiplication using arrays	☐	
C12	understands relationship between finding area and multiplying	☐	
C13	knows multiplication facts for: 2, 3, 4	☐	
C14	divides: without remainders, with remainders	☐	
C15	reads and writes multiplication and division sentences	☐	
C16	estimates: sums, differences, products, quotients	☐	
C17	understands commutative properties: addition, multiplication	☐	

Problem Solving and Reasoning

			Notes
P1	develops rules by generalizing	☐	
P2	develops winning strategies	☐	
P3	builds on previous knowledge to solve new problems	☐	
P4	anticipates, predicts, and explains to solve problems	☐	
P5	describes finding solutions and alternate strategies	☐	
P6	applies understanding of probability when making decisions	☐	

© Houghton Mifflin Harcourt Publishing Company

+	0	1	2	3	4	5	6	7	8	9	10
0	0 + 0	1 + 0	2 + 0	3 + 0	4 + 0	5 + 0	6 + 0	7 + 0	8 + 0	9 + 0	10 + 0
1	0 + 1	1 + 1	2 + 1	3 + 1	4 + 1	5 + 1	6 + 1	7 + 1	8 + 1	9 + 1	10 + 1
2	0 + 2	1 + 2	2 + 2	3 + 2	4 + 2	5 + 2	6 + 2	7 + 2	8 + 2	9 + 2	10 + 2
3	0 + 3	1 + 3	2 + 3	3 + 3	4 + 3	5 + 3	6 + 3	7 + 3	8 + 3	9 + 3	10 + 3
4	0 + 4	1 + 4	2 + 4	3 + 4	4 + 4	5 + 4	6 + 4	7 + 4	8 + 4	9 + 4	10 + 4
5	0 + 5	1 + 5	2 + 5	3 + 5	4 + 5	5 + 5	6 + 5	7 + 5	8 + 5	9 + 5	10 + 5
6	0 + 6	1 + 6	2 + 6	3 + 6	4 + 6	5 + 6	6 + 6	7 + 6	8 + 6	9 + 6	10 + 6
7	0 + 7	1 + 7	2 + 7	3 + 7	4 + 7	5 + 7	6 + 7	7 + 7	8 + 7	9 + 7	10 + 7
8	0 + 8	1 + 8	2 + 8	3 + 8	4 + 8	5 + 8	6 + 8	7 + 8	8 + 8	9 + 8	10 + 8
9	0 + 9	1 + 9	2 + 9	3 + 9	4 + 9	5 + 9	6 + 9	7 + 9	8 + 9	9 + 9	10 + 9
10	0 + 10	1 + 10	2 + 10	3 + 10	4 + 10	5 + 10	6 + 10	7 + 10	8 + 10	9 + 10	10 + 10

© Houghton Mifflin Harcourt Publishing Company

×	1	2	3	4	5	6	7	8	9	10
1	1 ×1	2 ×1	3 ×1	4 ×1	5 ×1	6 ×1	7 ×1	8 ×1	9 ×1	10 ×1
2	1 ×2	2 ×2	3 ×2	4 ×2	5 ×2	6 ×2	7 ×2	8 ×2	9 ×2	10 ×2
3	1 ×3	2 ×3	3 ×3	4 ×3	5 ×3	6 ×3	7 ×3	8 ×3	9 ×3	10 ×3
4	1 ×4	2 ×4	3 ×4	4 ×4	5 ×4	6 ×4	7 ×4	8 ×4	9 ×4	10 ×4
5	1 ×5	2 ×5	3 ×5	4 ×5	5 ×5	6 ×5	7 ×5	8 ×5	9 ×5	10 ×5
6	1 ×6	2 ×6	3 ×6	4 ×6	5 ×6	6 ×6	7 ×6	8 ×6	9 ×6	10 ×6
7	1 ×7	2 ×7	3 ×7	4 ×7	5 ×7	6 ×7	7 ×7	8 ×7	9 ×7	10 ×7
8	1 ×8	2 ×8	3 ×8	4 ×8	5 ×8	6 ×8	7 ×8	8 ×8	9 ×8	10 ×8
9	1 ×9	2 ×9	3 ×9	4 ×9	5 ×9	6 ×9	7 ×9	8 ×9	9 ×9	10 ×9
10	1 ×10	2 ×10	3 ×10	4 ×10	5 ×10	6 ×10	7 ×10	8 ×10	9 ×10	10 ×10

© Houghton Mifflin Harcourt Publishing Company

Answer Keys

© Houghton Mifflin Harcourt Publishing Company

Pretest Answer Key

1. (circle) (circle) (heart)
2. 2
3. $\frac{1}{2}$
4. $5 + 6 = 11$
5. 4×6 and 6×4
6. 9
7. $3 \times 6 = 18$ or $6 \times 3 = 18$
8. 95
9. 80
10. $36 < 61$, $99 > 61$
11. 8
12. 12
13. inches
14. 16 in.
15. 30
16. 1:15
17. 66¢
18. 13,085
19. B
20. D
21. A
22. C
23. B
24. B
25. B
26. D
27. A
28. B
29. D
30. C

Tested Skills	Item Numbers	Every Day Counts Element(s)
Patterns	1, 19	Calendar, Counting Tape and Hundred Chart
Place value and rounding	9, 18, 23, 24	Counting Tape and Hundred Chart, Daily Depositor
Number relationships	10, 22	Computations and Connections, Counting Tape and Hundred Chart
Addition and subtraction	4, 8	Computations and Connections, Counting Tape and Hundred Chart
Multiplication and division	5, 6, 7	Computations and Connections, Counting Tape and Hundred Chart, Coin Counter
Geometric shapes and their characteristics	2, 14, 20, 21	Calendar
Problem-solving strategies and estimating	4, 30	Calendar, Daily Depositor
Fractions	3	Calendar, Measurement
Analyzing and presenting data	25	Graph
Probability	26	Graph
Solving problems with time	15, 16, 27	Clock
Solving problems involving money	17, 28, 29	Daily Depositor, Coin Counter
Measuring length and capacity (standard, metric)	11, 12, 13	Measurement

© Houghton Mifflin Harcourt Publishing Company

Winter Test Answer Key

1. 12, 15, 18
2.
3. 24, 26, 28
4. Each is a closed figure.
   Each has 3 straight sides.
   Each has 3 angles.
5. 7 + 6 or 6 + 7
6. 24 − 9 = 15
7. 17
8. 3
9. 27
10. 7
11. 53
12. (see graph)
13. $6\frac{1}{2}$ ft
14. 1 quarter, 2 dimes, 4 pennies
15. 2:10
16. 1:55
17. 15
18. C
19. A
20. B
21. C
22. A
23. C
24. B
25. D
26. C
27. A
28. C
29. B
30. B

Bikes Fixed by Mr. Tan

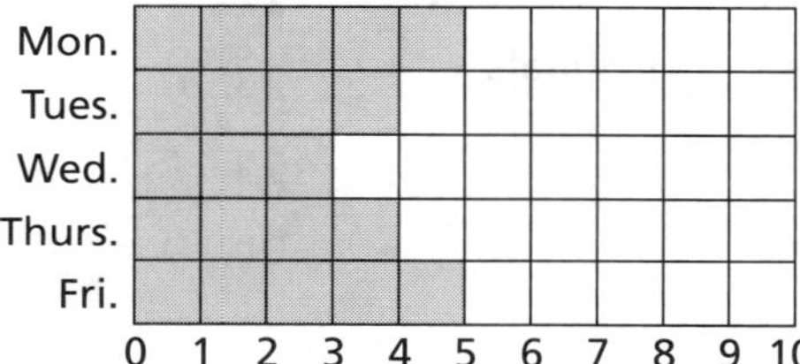

Number of Bikes

Tested Skills	Item Numbers	Every Day Counts Element(s)
Patterns	1, 2, 3, 28	Calendar, Counting Tape and Hundred Chart
Place value and rounding	10, 20, 21	Counting Tape and Hundred Chart, Daily Depositor
Number relationships	5, 19	Calendar, Computations and Connections
Addition and subtraction	7, 11	Computations and Connections, Counting Tape and Hundred Chart, Daily Depositor
Multiplication and division	29	Counting Tape and Hundred Chart
Geometric shapes and their characteristics	4, 18	Calendar
Problem-solving strategies and estimating	6, 9, 30	Calendar, Daily Depositor
Analyzing and presenting data	12	Graph
Probability	22	Graph
Solving problems with time	15, 16, 17, 25, 26	Clock
Solving problems involving money	14, 27	Daily Depositor, Coin Counter
Measuring length and capacity (standard, metric)	8, 13, 23, 24	Measurement

© Houghton Mifflin Harcourt Publishing Company

Spring Test Answer Key

1. 30, 36, 42
2. $\frac{1}{4}$
3. $2 \times 8 = 16$ or $8 \times 2 = 16$
4. 60
5. 4×9 and 9×4
6. 9:45
7. 3
8. 90
9. $83 > 54$ and $32 < 54$
10. 8, 12, 16, 20
11. 8,309
12. 4,000 + 200 + 50 + 1
13. 89¢
14. 63¢
15. 26¢
16.

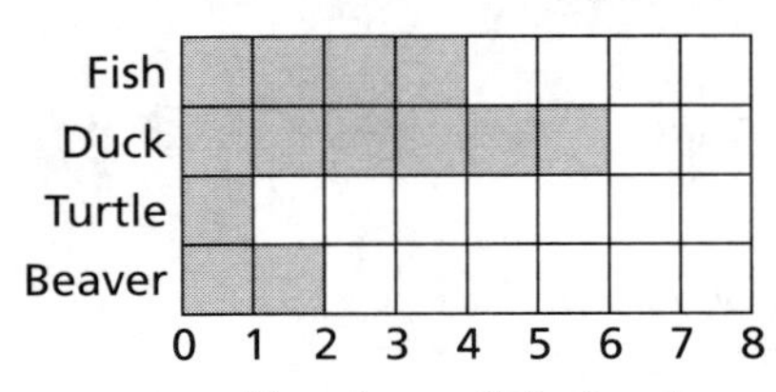

17. August
18. 7
19. C
20. A
21. C
22. D
23. B
24. C
25. C
26. A
27. B
28. A
29. B
30. D

Tested Skills	Item Numbers	Every Day Counts Element(s)
Patterns of numbers and multiples	1, 5, 10	Calendar, Counting Tape and Hundred Chart
Place value and rounding	8, 25, 26	Counting Tape and Hundred Chart
Number relationships and notations	9, 11, 12	Calendar, Computations and Connections, Daily Depositor
Fractions	2, 24	Calendar, Measurement
Geometric shapes and their characteristics	19, 20	Calendar
Problem-solving strategies and estimating	3, 21, 30	Calendar, Daily Depositor, Coin Counter
Analyzing and presenting data	16, 17, 18	Graph
Probability	29	Graph
Solving problems with time	4, 6, 22	Clock
Solving problems involving money	13, 14, 15, 27, 28	Daily Depositor, Coin Counter
Measuring length and perimeter	7, 23	Measurement

© Houghton Mifflin Harcourt Publishing Company

Post Test Answer Key

1. 
2. 2
3. $\frac{1}{3}$
4. 9 − 5 = 4
5. 8 × 4 and 4 × 8
6. 6
7. 3 × 5 = 15 or 5 × 3 = 15
8. 78
9. 80
10. 42 < 58, 70 > 58
11. 2
12. 4
13. yards
14. 9 sq. in.
15. 45
16. 3:45
17. 66¢
18. 24,809
19. B
20. C
21. A
22. D
23. C
24. A
25. D
26. A
27. D
28. B
29. C
30. B

Tested Skills	Item Numbers	Every Day Counts Element(s)
Patterns	1, 19	Calendar, Counting Tape and Hundred Chart
Place value and rounding	9, 18, 23, 24	Counting Tape and Hundred Chart, Daily Depositor
Number relationships	10, 22	Computations and Connections, Counting Tape and Hundred Chart
Addition and subtraction	4, 8	Computations and Connections, Counting Tape and Hundred Chart
Multiplication and division	5, 6, 7	Computations and Connections, Counting Tape and Hundred Chart, Coin Counter
Geometric shapes and their characteristics	2, 14, 20, 21	Calendar
Problem-solving strategies and estimating	4, 30	Calendar, Daily Depositor
Fractions	3	Calendar, Measurement
Analyzing and presenting data	25	Graph
Probability	26	Graph
Solving problems with time	15, 16, 27	Clock
Solving problems involving money	17, 28, 29	Daily Depositor, Coin Counter
Measuring length and capacity (standard, metric)	11, 12, 13	Measurement

© Houghton Mifflin Harcourt Publishing Company

MONTHLY ASSESSMENT

Use the calendar.

What do you notice about the:

1. the even numbered calendar pieces?

   They are all squares.

2. the odd numbered calendar pieces?

   They are all circles.

3. the pattern of small circles?

   They are multiples of 3.

4. the pattern of squares that stand on their corners?

   They are multiples of 4.

5. Count by 3s on the calendar. Which of these pieces are even numbers?

   6, 12, 18, 24, 30

6. Describe the calendar pattern for this month.

   Answers will vary: it is a circle square, circle square pattern;

   an ABAB pattern; every third piece has a small circle.

Complete the patterns:

7. 3, 6, 9, 12, 15, 18, 21.

8. 4, 8, 12, 16, 20, 24, 28.

MONTHLY ASSESSMENT

1. List all the doubles facts from 5 + 5 to 10 + 10.

   5 + 5 = 10

   6 + 6 = 12

   7 + 7 = 14

   8 + 8 = 16

   9 + 9 = 18

   10 + 10 = 20

2. List all the doubles plus 1 facts from 5 + 6 to 10 + 11.

   5 + 6 = 11

   6 + 7 = 13

   7 + 8 = 15

   8 + 9 = 17

   9 + 10 = 19

   10 + 11 = 21

Add.

3. 11 + 12 = 23
4. 15 + 16 = 31
5. 20 + 21 = 41
6. 30 + 31 = 61
7. 50 + 51 = 101
8. 100 + 101 = 201

© Houghton Mifflin Harcourt Publishing Company

MONTHLY ASSESSMENT

Complete the pattern on the calendar.

By recreating the calendar pattern, students may discover new connections or patterns they didn't notice earlier. Check student work against the completed calendar pattern on page 11.

MONTHLY ASSESSMENT

1. There are 4 cups in a quart.
   How many cups are there in 2 quarts? 8
2. How many cups are there in 3 quarts? 12
3. How many cups are there in 4 quarts? 16
4. There are 2 cups in a pint.
   How many pints are there in 1 quart? 2
5. How many pints are there in 3 quarts? 6
6. What time is shown on the clock? 3:15
7. What time will it be 15 minutes later? 3:30
8. What time will it be one half hour after that? 4:00
9. Draw hands on the clock to show that time.

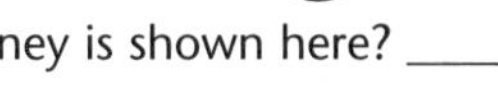
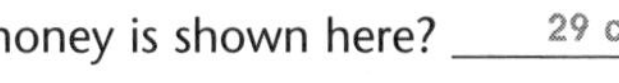

10. How much money is shown here? 29 cents
11. What single coin is equal in value to two dimes and one nickel? one quarter
12. How many nickels does it take to equal the value of two dimes? four
13. How many dimes does it take to equal the value of two quarters? five

© Houghton Mifflin Harcourt Publishing Company

ANSWER KEY

MONTHLY ASSESSMENT

Use the calendar.

1. Which calendar pieces have big circles on them?

   5, 10, 15, 20, 25, 30

   What do you notice about this pattern?

   They are all multiples of 5.

2. Which calendar pieces have small circles on them?

   2, 4, 6, 8, 10, 12, 14

   What do you notice about this pattern?

   They are all even numbers.

3. What is different between the triangles on the numbers 1, 3, 6, 8 and those on 2, 4, 7, 9?

   The ones on the first set of numbers have all sides equal or congruent, the second set have only two sides equal

4. Complete the pattern on the calendar.

5. Suppose the first Sunday of the month is a big circle. What day of the week will be the next big circle? Why?

   Friday, it is 5 days later.

Continue these patterns.

6. 10, 20, 30, 40, 50, 60, 70, 80
7. 45, 40, 35, 30, 25, 20, 15, 10, 5
8. 10, 15, 25, 30, 40, 45, 55, 60, 70

MONTHLY ASSESSMENT

Add.

1. 8 + 8 = 16
2. 8 + 9 = 17
3. 8 + 7 = 15
4. 6 + 5 = 11
5. 7 + 6 = 13
6. 9 + 10 = 19

Subtract.

7. 15 − 7 = 8
8. 15 − 8 = 7
9. 12 − 6 = 6
10. 17 − 9 = 8
11. 18 − 9 = 9
12. 13 − 7 = 6

Add or Subtract.

13. 8 + 10 = 18
14. 36 − 10 = 26
15. 36 − 20 = 16
16. 30 + 9 = 39
17. 50 + 6 = 56
18. 77 − 40 = 37

Fill in the missing numbers.

19. 30 − 16 = 14
20. 31 − 16 = 15
21. 44 − 20 = 24
22. 36 − 10 = 26
23. 53 − 20 = 33
24. 53 − 30 = 23
25. 81 − 40 = 41
26. 50 + 8 = 58
27. 40 + 9 = 49

55  85 37  60 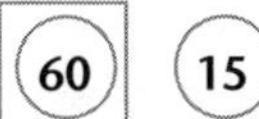 15 67  20 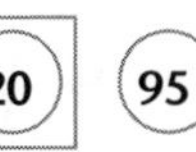 95 44

28. Draw a box around the numbers you say when counting by 10's.
29. Draw a ring around the numbers you say when counting by 5's.

© Houghton Mifflin Harcourt Publishing Company

ANSWER KEY

MONTHLY ASSESSMENT

1. In Mathville, Mrs. Neville, Mr. Garcia, and Mrs. Wilson are third-grade teachers. There are 76 third-grade students in the school. Mrs. Neville's class has 26 students. Mr. Garcia's class has 25 students. How many students are there all together in these two classrooms? 51
2. How many students are in Mrs. Wilson's classroom? 25
3. Yesterday we had $465.00 in the Daily Depositor. Today we will add $31.00. How much money will we have then? $496.00
4. How much more money do we need to have $600.00? $104.00
5. There are 24 students in a class. They need to make even teams to compete in the school spelling bee. How many different ways can they make even teams? List all the possibilities.

There are 6 ways. They could make two teams of 12 students, three teams of 8 students, four teams of 6 students, six teams of 4 students, eight teams of 3 students, or twelve teams of 2 students. Encourage students to make an organized list to solve this problem.

Fill in the table.

	Quarters	Dimes	Nickels
6. Make 60¢ using 3 coins.	2	1	0
7. Make 60¢ using 4 coins.	2	0	2
8. Make 60¢ using 5 coins.	1	3	1
9. Make 60¢ using 6 coins.	1	2	3
10. Make 60¢ using 7 coins.	1	1	5
11. Make 60¢ using 8 coins.	1	0	7

Check students' answers for accuracy.
There are solutions other than those shown here.

MONTHLY ASSESSMENT

1. Draw hands on the first clock to show 8:00.
2. Draw hands on the second clock to show the time ten minutes later.
3. Draw hands on the third clock to show the time twenty minutes after that.

For each problem, decide if it is A.M. or P.M.
Draw a ring around your answer.

4. The clock shows 6:00. You are eating dinner. A.M. (P.M.)
5. The clock shows 10:00. You are at school. (A.M.) P.M.
6. The clock shows 12:00. You are eating lunch. A.M. (P.M.)

Draw a ring around the best answer.

7. Which unit would you use to measure the distance from one city to another?
   yard (mile)
8. Which unit would you use to measure the weight of a dog?
   ounce (pound)
9. Which unit would you use to measure the length of a pencil?
   (inch) foot

10. Draw a box around the triangle.
11. Draw a ring around the square.

© Houghton Mifflin Harcourt Publishing Company

ANSWER KEY

MONTHLY ASSESSMENT

Use the calendar.

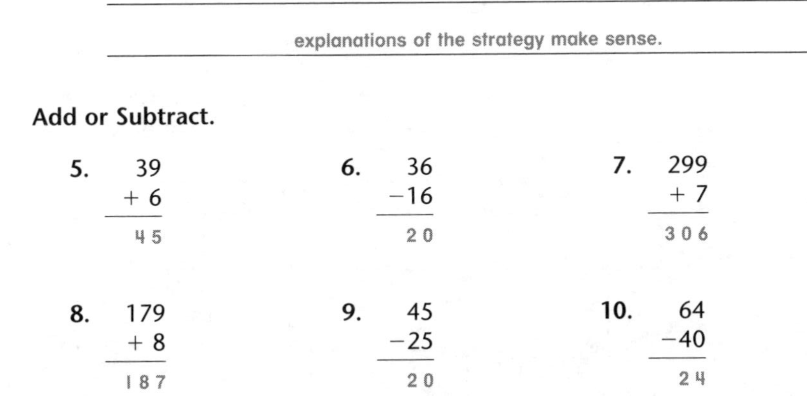

1. What do you notice about the pieces that have circles on them?

   Even numbers

2. What is an even number?

   A number that is a multiple of 2.

3. Describe the calendar pattern this month. Answers will vary:

   rectangle, square, rhombus that rotates 90° with every repeat, and dots on every even number.

4. Complete the pattern on the calendar.

5. Which rhombuses have circles on them? Why?

   6, 12, 18, 24, 30, they are the even multiples of 3, or multiples of 6.

6. How are the square and rhombus different? The square has right angles.

7. How are the rectangle on the 1st and the rectangle on the 4th different?

   It is rotated 90°.

Complete the patterns.

8. 5, 11, 17, 23, 29, 35, 41.

9. 3, 9, 15, 21, 27, 33

MONTHLY ASSESSMENT

1. Write and solve three problems that add nine to a number.

   + ______ + ______ + ______

2. Explain how you solved these problems.

   Answers will vary. Make sure students' explanations of the strategy make sense.

3. Write and solve three problems that subtract nine from a number.

   – ______ – ______ – ______

4. Explain how you solved these problems.

   Answers will vary. Make sure students' explanations of the strategy make sense.

Add or Subtract.

5. $39 + 6 = 45$
6. $36 - 16 = 20$
7. $299 + 7 = 306$
8. $179 + 8 = 187$
9. $45 - 25 = 20$
10. $64 - 40 = 24$

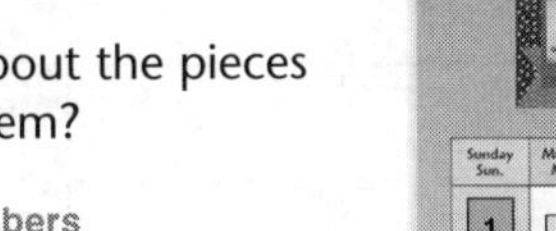

© Houghton Mifflin Harcourt Publishing Company

MONTHLY ASSESSMENT

The students in Mathville sold pencils, rulers, pens, and markers to raise money for their school. The table shows how many of each item they sold for two days. Use the table to answer the questions.

	Friday	Saturday
pencils	20	48
rulers	2	10
pens	19	33
markers	9	26

1. How many pencils did they sell all together? 68
2. How many more markers did they sell on Saturday than on Friday? 17
3. How many pens did they sell all together? 52
4. Which item did they sell the fewest of? rulers
5. Which item did they sell the most of? pencils
6. How many markers did they sell all together? 35
7. On which day did they sell more items? Saturday
8. Kiesha keeps all her marbles in a box. She has 10 blue marbles, 5 red marbles, 7 green marbles, and 3 yellow marbles. How many marbles does she have all together? 25
9. If she reaches into the box and pulls out one marble without looking, what color marble is she most likely to pull out?
   a blue marble
10. Explain your thinking. Answers will vary. Students should realize that pulling out a blue marble is most likely because there are more of them.

MONTHLY ASSESSMENT

1. Name three things in your classroom that you think are about one foot long.
   Answers will vary.
2. Name three things in your classroom that you think are about one yard long.
   Answers will vary.
3. Name three things in your house that you think are about one yard long.
   Answers will vary.

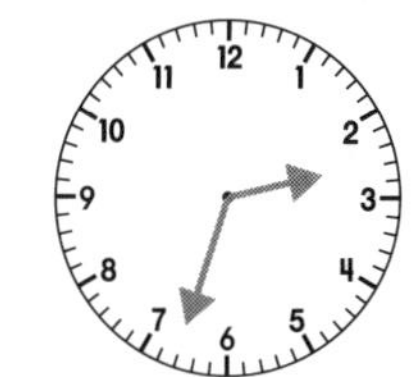

4. Draw hands on the clock showing the same time displayed on the digital clock.
5. What time will it be 30 minutes later? 3:03
6. There are three feet in one yard. How many feet are there in three yards? 9
7. How many feet are there in five yards? 15
8. There are twelve inches in one foot. How many inches are there in two feet? 24
9. How many inches are there in $\frac{1}{2}$ foot? 6

© Houghton Mifflin Harcourt Publishing Company

ANSWER KEY

MONTHLY ASSESSMENT

Use the calendar.

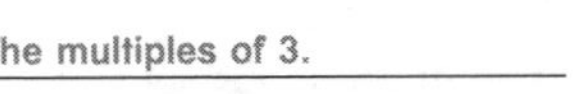

1. Describe the pattern for this month?

   Answers will vary: it repeats, trapezoid, trapezoid, hexagon. The second trapezoid is a reflection or a flip of the first one. Every 6th day there is a star.

2. Which calendar pieces have hexagons?

   The multiples of 3.

3. Which hexagons have stars?

   The even multiples of 3, or the multiples of 6.

4. How can the first trapezoid be made into the second trapezoid?

   It can be flipped or reflected.

5. If the area of the hexagon is 1 square unit, what is the area of the trapezoid?

   $\frac{1}{2}$ of the square unit or $\frac{1}{2}$ of the trapezoid.

6. How many halves make 2 wholes? 4

Complete the patterns:

7. 6, 12, 18, 24, 30, 36, 42
8. 1, 2, 4, 5, 7, 8, 10, 11, 13, 14, 16
9. 27, 21, 15, 9, 3, ?

MONTHLY ASSESSMENT

Add or Subtract.

1. 7 + 5 = 12
2. 14 − 8 = 6
3. 19 − 10 = 9
4. 4 + 9 = 13
5. 16 − 9 = 7
6. 17 − 9 = 8
7. 18 − 9 = 9
8. 13 − 7 = 6
9. 8 + 7 = 15

Add. Encourage students to use a variety of strategies to solve these problems. Some can be done mentally while others will require paper and pencil.

10. 56 + 56 = 112
11. 143 + 47 = 190
12. 300 + 437 = 737
13. 250 + 101 = 351
14. 77 + 73 = 150
15. 311 + 199 = 510
16. 634 + 512 = 1146
17. 19 + 321 = 340
18. 210 + 456 = 666

Subtract.

19. 80 − 23 = 57
20. 465 − 256 = 209
21. 712 − 310 = 402
22. 173 − 85 = 88
23. 840 − 326 = 514
24. 35 − 17 = 18
25. 505 − 26 = 479
26. 47 − 19 = 28
27. 621 − 223 = 398

© Houghton Mifflin Harcourt Publishing Company

ANSWER KEY

MONTHLY ASSESSMENT

Use the digits 2, 3, 4, 5, and 6 to make the sums side to side (horizontally) and up and down (vertically).

(6) / (5)(2)(4) / (3)

(2) / (3)(4)(5) / (6)

(5) / (3)(6)(4) / (2)

1. Make the sum 11.
2. What number is in the middle circle? 2
3. Make the sum 12.
4. What number is in the middle circle? 4
5. Make the sum 13.
6. What number is in the middle circle? 6
7. What is the pattern of the numbers in the middle circle? The number in the middle increases by 2 each time; the lowest digit goes in the middle to make the smallest sum.

Try using the digits 3, 4, 5, 6, and 7.

(7) / (6)(3)(5) / (4)

(3) / (6)(5)(4) / (7)

(6) / (4)(7)(5) / (3)

8. Make the sum 14.
9. What number is in the middle circle? 3
10. Make the sum 15.
11. What number is in the middle circle? 5
12. Make the sum 16.
13. What number is in the middle circle? 7
14. Write two addition sentences and two subtraction sentences that equal the number of the new year.

Answers will vary. If the new year is 2000, the following are acceptable responses:

1990 + 10 = 2000; 1900 + 100 = 2000; 2100 − 100 = 2000; 3000 − 1000 = 2000.

MONTHLY ASSESSMENT

1. If each side of the triangle is one inch long, how many inches long are the sides of the triangle all together? 3
2. If each side of the square is two inches long, how many inches long are the sides of the square all together? 8
3. How many sides does the star have? 10
4. If each side of the star is one inch long, how many inches long are the sides of the star all together? 10
5. Rosa went to the store and bought an eraser for 71¢. She paid with a one-dollar bill. How much change did she get back?

   29¢
6. What is the least number of coins you could use to make that amount? 5
7. What coins are they? 1 quarter and 4 pennies
8. Write another way to make that amount.

   Answers will vary. Check that students' solutions equal 29 cents.
9. How many minutes past the hour is it? 36
10. What hour is it? 3 o'clock
11. What time is it? Thirty-six minutes past three or 3:36
12. How many minutes until the next hour? 24
13. What time will it be then? 4 o'clock

© Houghton Mifflin Harcourt Publishing Company

ANSWER KEY

MONTHLY ASSESSMENT

Use the calendar.

1. Describe the pattern this month.
   Answers will vary: it repeats; rectangular prism, cube, cylinder, pyramid, cone, sphere.

2. How many days does it take to make a complete pattern? 6

3. January has 31 days. How many complete patterns will there be in January?
   5

4. How many more days will be left? 1

What do you notice about the pieces that have:

5. spheres on them? They are multiples of 6.

7. cylinders on them? They are multiples of 3.

Circle the correct letter.

8. Cubes have:
   a. curved edges. (b.) 6 square faces. c. no square faces.

9. Cylinders have:
   a. 4 circle bases. (b.) a curved surface. c. 2 corners.

10. Why are the spheres arranged diagonally to the left on the calendar?
    The pattern repeats every 6 days, one less than the number of days that repeat every 7 days on a calendar.

MONTHLY ASSESSMENT

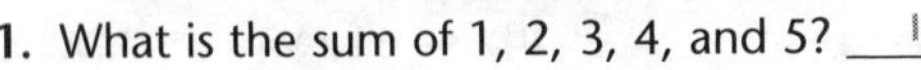

1. What is the sum of 1, 2, 3, 4, and 5? 15

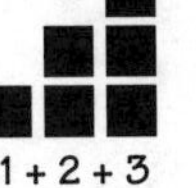
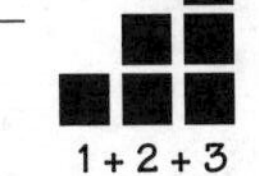

2. What is a fast way of adding these numbers?
   Multiply the middle number (3) by the number of consecutive numbers (5) to get 15.

3. What is the sum of 11, 12, and 13? 36

4. What is a fast way of adding these numbers? Multiply the middle number (12) by the number of consecutive numbers (3) to get 36.

5. What is the sum of 13, 14, 15, 16, and 17? 75

6. What is a fast way of adding these numbers? Multiply the middle number (15) by the number of consecutive numbers (5) to get 75.

7. What is the sum of all the numbers from 1 to 10? 55

8. Tell how you got your answer. Encourage a variety of strategies for doing this, including the visual models. Some students may find tens; others will find friendly combinations. Accept all of these solutions.

Multiply.

9. $2 \times 8 =$ 16
10. $3 \times 8 =$ 24
11. $7 \times 2 =$ 14
12. $7 \times 3 =$ 21
13. $3 \times 5 =$ 15
14. $2 \times 5 =$ 10

© Houghton Mifflin Harcourt Publishing Company

Monthly Assessment

I'm a Number. . .

15	16	17	18	19	(20)	21	22	23	24	25	26	27	28	29	(30)	31	32	33	34	35	36	37	38	39	(40)	41

Look at the Counting Tape to answer these riddles.

1. I'm an even number between 20 and 40. Both my digits are the same. Who am I? 22
2. I'm the smallest number that rounds to 40 when you round me to the nearest 10. Who am I? 35
3. I'm an odd number between 30 and 40. The sum of my digits is 12. Who am I? 39
4. I'm a number between 20 and 29 that you say when you count by 2's and when you count by 3's. Who am I? 24
5. I'm the number you get when you round 32 to the nearest ten. Who am I? 30

Solve these problems.

6. In a school survey about favorite colors, 39 students liked red and 56 liked blue. How many more students liked blue than red? 17
7. In a third-grade classroom at another school, there are twice as many girls as boys. There are 7 boys in the class. How many students are in the class all together? 21
8. How did you get your answer? Answers will vary.
   7 boys times 2 equals 14 girls; 14 plus 7 equals 21 students all together.

Monthly Assessment

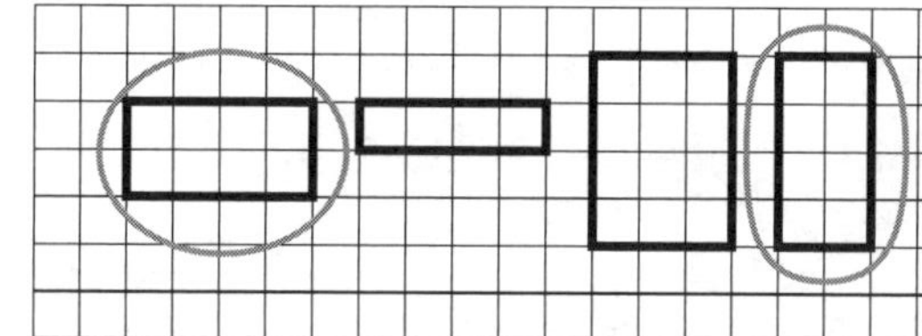

1. What time does the clock show? 8:22
2. What time will it be in 10 minutes? 8:32
3. What time was it 20 minutes ago? 8:02
4. How many minutes until the next hour? 38
5. What time will it be then? 9:00
6. If the time is A.M., is it closer to breakfast time or dinner time? breakfast time
7. What is the least number of coins you need to make 91 cents if you don't use a half-dollar? 6
8. What coins did you use? 3 quarters, 1 dime, 1 nickel, and 1 penny

9. Draw a ring around the two rectangles that are the same size and shape.
10. How many sides are there on two rectangles? 8
11. How many sides are there on four rectangles? 16
12. How many sides are there on eight rectangles? 32

© Houghton Mifflin Harcourt Publishing Company

MONTHLY ASSESSMENT

Use the calendar.

February

Sunday Sun.	Monday Mon.	Tuesday Tues.	Wednesday Wed.	Thursday Thurs.	Friday Fri.	Saturday Sat.
	1	2	3	4	5	6
7	8	9	10	11	12	13
14	15	16	17	18	19	

1. What fraction follows this pattern on the calendar? 2, 6, 10, 14, 18? $\frac{1}{2}$

2. What is the number pattern for the pieces with $\frac{1}{3}$ of the circle shaded?
   3, 7, 11, 15, 19, 23, 27
   What fraction of a $\frac{1}{3}$ circle is not shaded? $\frac{2}{3}$

3. How many days does it take to make a complete pattern? 4

4. February has 28 days. How many times will the pattern repeat? 7

5. Will the pieces that are one whole ever repeat more than 7 times?
   When? Yes, on a leap year.

6. Which is larger, $\frac{1}{3}$ or $\frac{1}{4}$? Why? $\frac{1}{3}$, dividing a circle into three equal parts means the parts are bigger than if they were divided into four equal parts.

7. Suppose the pattern continued on.
   What fraction will be on the next Friday? $\frac{1}{2}$

8. Suppose the pattern continued on.
   Which pieces would have the next three $\frac{1}{4}$ on them? 32, 36, 40.

9. Why are the $\frac{1}{4}$ pieces arranged diagonally to the right on the calendar?
   Answers will vary: the pattern repeats every 4 days, twice that is 8 days. This is one more than the repeating pattern of weeks on a calendar.

MONTHLY ASSESSMENT

1. Describe a fast way of adding 99, 100, and 101. Accept a variety of strategies. One strategy is to multiply the middle number by the number of consecutive numbers in the list.

2. What is the sum? 300

3. What is the sum of 97, 98, 99, 100, 101, and 102? 597

4. Describe how you got your answer. Accept a variety of strategies. Some students may see two groups of three consecutive numbers, apply the middle number multiplication strategy, and add the two amounts. Others may make three pairs of numbers that total 199 and add them to get the total.

What Number Am I?

5. I am the number of quarters in ten dollars. What number am I? 40
6. I am the number of legs on six chairs. What number am I? 24
7. I am the number of cups in two quarts. What number am I? 8
8. I am the number of quarts in five gallons. What number am I? 20
9. I am the number of tires on eight cars. What number am I? 32
10. I am the number of cups in one gallon. What number am I? 16
11. I am the number of legs on seven cats. What number am I? 28
12. I am the number of sides on nine squares. What number am I? 36
13. I am the number of feet in four yards. What number am I? 12

Subtract. Try to do these mentally.

14. $5764 - 101 = 5663$
15. $5764 - 199 = 5565$
16. $3205 - 99 = 3106$
17. $3205 - 299 = 2906$

© Houghton Mifflin Harcourt Publishing Company

MONTHLY ASSESSMENT

Use the Hundreds Chart to help you.

1	2	3	4	5	6	7	8	9	10
11	12	13	14	15	16	17	18	19	20
21	22	23	24	25	26	27	28	29	30
31	32	33	34	35	36	37	38	39	40
41	42	43	44	45	46	47	48	49	50
51	52	53	54	55	56	57	58	59	60
61	62	63	64	65	66	67	68	69	70
71	72	73	74	75	76	77	78	79	80
81	82	83	84	85	86	87	88	89	90
91	92	93	94	95	96	97	98	99	100

1. When rounding to the nearest ten, what is the largest number that rounds to 90? 94
2. When rounding to the nearest ten, what is the smallest number that rounds to 90? 85
3. When rounding to the nearest ten, what number will 96 round to? 100
4. Explain your thinking. Accept a variety of strategies for this problem.
5. What number is exactly halfway between 90 and 100? 95
6. Look at the numbers between 80 and 100. When rounding to the nearest ten, do more of these numbers round up or down? Up
7. Explain your thinking. Eight numbers, 81 through 84 and 91 through 94, round down. Ten numbers, 85 through 89 and 95 through 99, round up.

Think of the numbers you say when you count by 5's. Then think of the numbers you say when you count by 10's.

8. What is the first number you say when counting by both 5's and 10's? 10
9. When you count by both 5's and 10's, are the numbers you say even or odd numbers? Even
10. How do you know? This is a difficult problem because it is not asking students for a specific number but for a characteristic of all numbers that are multiples of both five and ten, namely that they must be even.

MONTHLY ASSESSMENT

1. Imagine you have a stack of 100 pennies. How many centimeters high do you estimate the stack would be? Answers will vary.
2. Stack ten pennies, measure the stack, and calculate how many centimeters high a stack of 100 pennies would be. Write your answer and explain how you figured it out.
   15 centimeters high. Ten pennies are about 1.5 centimeters tall, so 10 groups of ten pennies would be 15 centimeters high.
3. Compare your answer to problems 1 and 2.
   Was your estimate close? ______
4. How many sides are there on this star? 10
5. How many sides are there on two stars? 20

Try this.

6. How many sides are there on five stars? 50

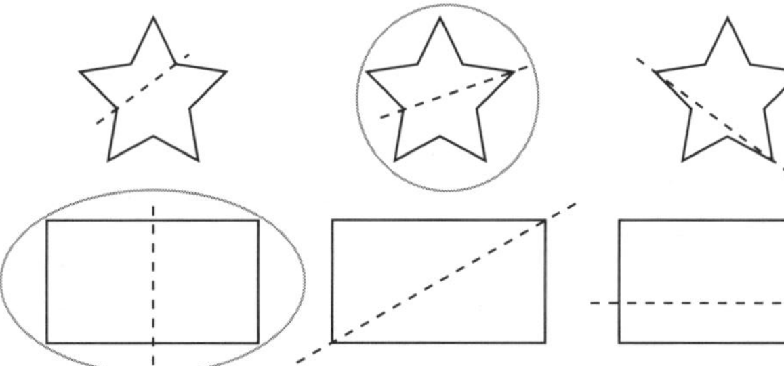

Only one of these stars and one of these rectangles show true lines of symmetry.

7. Draw a ring around the star that shows a true line of symmetry.
8. Draw a ring around the rectangle that shows a true line of symmetry.

© Houghton Mifflin Harcourt Publishing Company

ANSWER KEY

MONTHLY ASSESSMENT

1. Draw figure 5 in this pattern and fill in the blank below it. 25

2. Draw figure 6 in the pattern and fill in the blank below it. 36

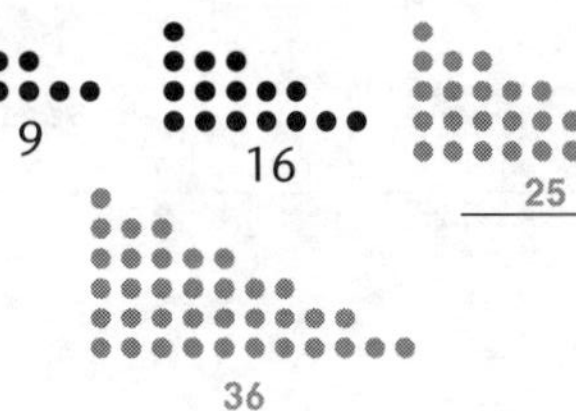

3. Figure 1 has how many dots? 1
4. Figure 2 has how many dots? 4
5. Figure 3 has how many dots? 9
6. Figure 4 has how many dots? 16
7. What is the relationship between each figure number and how many dots are in the figure? The number of dots is the number of the figure times that same number, or the number of dots is the square of the figure number.
8. How many dots will be in figure 7? 49
9. How many dots are added to figure 1 to make figure 2? 3
10. How many dots are added to figure 2 to make figure 3? 5
11. How many dots are added to figure 3 to make figure 4? 7
12. How many dots are added to figure 4 to make figure 5? 9
13. What do you notice about the number of dots that are added each time? They are consecutive odd numbers.
14. How many dots will be added to figure 6 to make figure 7? 13

MONTHLY ASSESSMENT

Draw an "X" on all the numbers you say when you count by fives.

1	2	3	4	5	6	7	8	9	10
11	12	13	14	15	16	17	18	19	20
21	22	23	24	25	26	27	28	29	30
31	32	33	34	35	36	37	38	39	40
41	42	43	44	45	46	47	48	49	50
51	52	53	54	55	56	57	58	59	60
61	62	63	64	65	66	67	68	69	70
71	72	73	74	75	76	77	78	79	80
81	82	83	84	85	86	87	88	89	90
91	92	93	94	95	96	97	98	99	100

1. What do you notice about these numbers? They all show up in two columns; they all end with a zero or a five.

Draw a ring on all the numbers you say when you count by tens.

2. What do you notice about these numbers? They all show up in one column; they all end with a zero; they are all even numbers.
3. What is the first number you say when you count by threes and tens? 30
4. What is the first number you say when you count by fours and tens? 40
5. What is the first number you say when you count by threes, fours, and tens? 60

Multiply.

6. $7 \times 5 =$ 35
7. $6 \times 10 =$ 60
8. $9 \times 10 =$ 90
9. $5 \times 4 =$ 20
10. $3 \times 5 =$ 15
11. $10 \times 10 =$ 100
12. $6 \times 5 =$ 30
13. $7 \times 10 =$ 70
14. $8 \times 5 =$ 40
15. $5 \times 5 =$ 25
16. $10 \times 3 =$ 30
17. $10 \times 5 =$ 50
18. $9 \times 5 =$ 45
19. $8 \times 10 =$ 80
20. $4 \times 10 =$ 40

© Houghton Mifflin Harcourt Publishing Company

MONTHLY ASSESSMENT

1. There are 24 students in the class. One fourth of them have blond hair. One half of them have brown hair. The rest have black hair. How many students have blond hair? 6
2. How many students have brown hair? 12
3. How many students have black hair? 6
4. How did you get your answers? Answers will vary. Students should demonstrate their understanding that 24 can be broken up into 4 groups of 6, and one of these groups is one fourth. 24 can also be broken up into 2 groups of 12, and one of those groups is one half.
5. In the same class, one third of the students are girls. How many boys are in the class? 16
6. Describe how you got your answer, Answers will vary. Students should demonstrate that 24 can be broken up into 3 groups of 8, and one of those groups is one third. Then, 24 − 8 = 16.

Round these numbers to the nearest hundred.

7. 6213 rounds to 6200
8. 6166 rounds to 6200
9. What do you notice about your answers? They are the same.
10. What is the smallest number that rounds to 7200 when rounded to the nearest hundred? 7150
11. What is the largest number that rounds to 7400 when rounded to the nearest hundred? 7449
12. A number rounds to 7100 when rounded to the nearest hundred. What could the number be? Any number between 7050 and 7149 rounds to 7100.
13. A number rounds to 7000 when rounded to the to he nearest hundred. It is greater than 7020. What number could it be? Any number between 7021 and 7049 rounds to 7000.

Make sure students understand that in each of the last two problems, there is a range of numbers from which to choose.

MONTHLY ASSESSMENT

1. Show one half on each of these figures. You can draw a line or color part of each figure with your pencil.
Check student work. There are solutions other than the ones shown here.
2. Draw a ring around one half of these circles.
3. Draw a ring around one half of these squares.
4. Draw a ring around one fourth of theses circles.
5. Draw a ring around one fourth of these squares.

Solve these coin puzzles. Don't use half-dollars.

6. Fred has five coins worth 80 cents. What coins does he have? 2 quarters and 3 dimes.
7. Amy wants to make $1.16 (116 cents) three different ways. How can she do it using 7 coins? 4 quarters, 1 dime, 1 nickel, and 1 penny
8. How can she do it using 10 coins? 2 quarters, 6 dimes, 1 nickel, and 1 penny; or 3 quarters, 2 dimes, 4 nickels, and 1 penny.
9. How can she do it using 13 coins? 11 dimes, 1 nickel, and 1 penny; or 3 quarters, 3 dimes, 1 nickel, and 6 pennies.

Students should use the information from problem 7 to solve problems 8 and 9. The hope is that students will keep the 1 nickel and 1 penny constant for each solution and convert 2 quarters to 5 dimes in the last two problems. This increases the number of coins used by 3 each time. There are other ways to solve these problems. Accept any correct solutions.

© Houghton Mifflin Harcourt Publishing Company

ANSWER KEY

MONTHLY ASSESSMENT

Use the calendar for problems 1–8

1. Describe the pattern on the calendar.

   Answers will vary: it repeats: square, square, trapezoid, rectangle, rectangle, heart.

2. How are a trapezoid and a rectangle alike? How are they different?

   Both have four sides, are closed figures, and have one set of parallel sides. A rectangle must have two sets of parallel sides and four right angles.

3. How many lines of symmetry does a rectangle have? 2

4. Draw the lines of symmetry for this square.

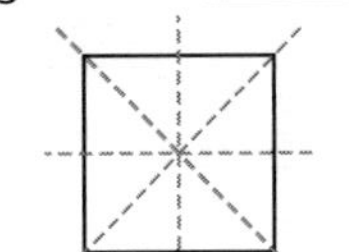

Look at the first six pieces on the calendar.

5. Write a fraction for the number of these pieces that have squares on them. $\frac{2}{6}$ or $\frac{1}{3}$

6. Write a fraction for the number of these pieces that do not have squares on them. $\frac{4}{6}$ or $\frac{2}{3}$

7. Write a division sentence to show how many times this pattern will repeat during the month.

   30 ÷ 6 = 5

8. Suppose this pattern continued on. Which pieces would have the next three hearts on them? 36, 42, 48

MONTHLY ASSESSMENT

For problems 1–12, check student responses for accuracy.

Number sentences for the 30th day of April.
Write three number sentences that equal 30. Use only addition.

1. ______ + ______ = 30 2. ______ + ______ = 30

3. ______ + ______ = 30

Write three number sentences that equal 30 using only subtraction.

4. ______ − ______ = 30 5. ______ − ______ = 30

6. ______ − ______ = 30

Write three number sentences that equal 30 using only multiplication.

7. ______ × ______ = 30 8. ______ × ______ = 30

9. ______ × ______ = 30

Write three number sentences that equal 30 using multiplication and then addition. For example, 1 × 2 + 28 = 30.

10. ______ × ______ + ______ = 30

11. ______ × ______ + ______ = 30

12. ______ × ______ + ______ = 30

Divide. If there is no remainder, write a zero after the R.

13. 25 ÷ 5 = 5 R 0 14. 26 ÷ 5 = 5 R 1

15. 13 ÷ 6 = 2 R 1 16. 18 ÷ 6 = 3 R 0

17. 18 ÷ 4 = 4 R 2 18. 19 ÷ 2 = 9 R 1

19. 20 ÷ 4 = 5 R 0 20. 20 ÷ 3 = 6 R 2

© Houghton Mifflin Harcourt Publishing Company

MONTHLY ASSESSMENT

1. Lin has 21 toothpicks. She makes some triangles and some squares with the toothpicks. How many of each shape can she make if she uses all 21 toothpicks?

   3 triangles and 3 squares

2. Danny has 30 toothpicks. How many triangles can he make using all 30 toothpicks? 10

3. Will he have any toothpicks left over? If so, how many? No

4. If Danny makes only squares, how many can he make? 7

5. Will he have any toothpicks left over? If so, how many? Yes; 2

6. Draw rings around the two rectangles that are divided into four equal parts.

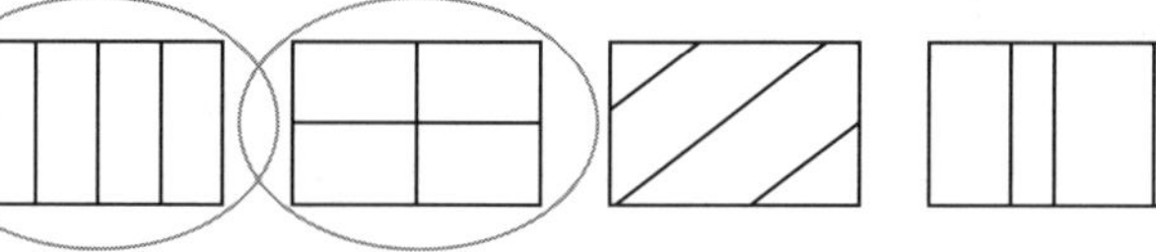

7. At the store, large stickers cost $0.25 each, medium stickers cost $0.15 each, and small stickers cost $0.06 each. How much money will you spend if you buy 3 large stickers, 5 medium stickers, and 10 small stickers?

   $2.10

8. If you pay for your stickers with a five-dollar bill, how much change will you get back?

   $2.90

MONTHLY ASSESSMENT

1. How many minutes are in $\frac{1}{2}$ hour? 30
2. How many minutes are in $1\frac{1}{2}$ hours? 90
3. How many minutes are in $\frac{1}{4}$ hour? 15
4. How many minutes are in $1\frac{3}{4}$ hours? 105
5. What time is shown on the clock? 2:00
6. What time will it be 4 hours from that time? 6:00
7. What time was it 1 hour earlier than that time? 1:00

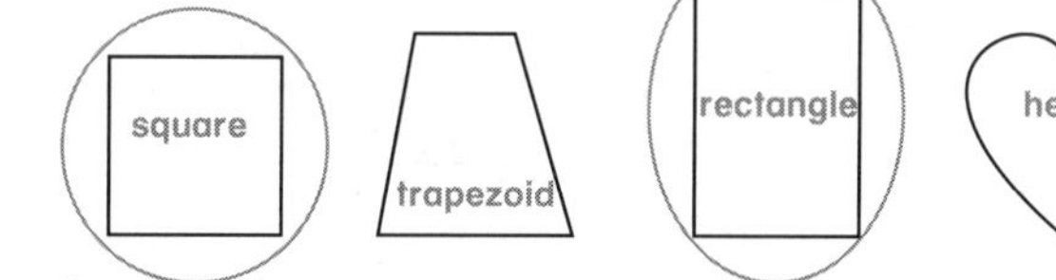

8. Write the name of each shape inside the figure.
9. Which one of these shapes has no parallel sides? heart
10. Draw rings around the shapes that have two pairs of parallel opposite sides.
11. Which figure has four equal sides? the square
12. Which two shapes have square corners? the square and the rectangle
13. How many ounces are in $\frac{1}{2}$ pound? 8
14. How many ounces are in $2\frac{1}{2}$ pounds? 40
15. How many ounces are in $\frac{1}{4}$ pound? 4
16. How many ounces are in $1\frac{3}{4}$ pounds? 28

© Houghton Mifflin Harcourt Publishing Company

MONTHLY ASSESSMENT

Use the calendar.

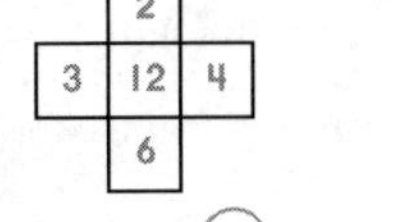

1. What are the shapes on the calendar? How are they alike?

   A cone, a ball and a cylinder.

   They all have curved surfaces.

2. Describe this pattern using letters.

   AABBCC

4. Write a division sentence to show how many times this pattern will repeat during the month. Is there a remainder?

   31 ÷ 6 = 5 r. 1

5. Suppose this pattern continued on. What shape would be on 38? Why?

   Cone, Answers will vary: the vertical pattern is the same as the horizontal one.

What shape am I?

6. I have two parallel bases and a curved surface connecting them.

   a. sphere b. cone (c.) cylinder

7. I have one circle base and a curved surface.

   a. sphere (b.) cone c. cylinder

8. What is another real world example of each shape on the calendar?

Cone	Cylinder	Sphere
Answers will vary.	Answers will vary.	Answers will vary.

MONTHLY ASSESSMENT

Add. Try to solve these problems mentally.

1. 205 + 85 = 290
2. 945 + 70 = 1015
3. 680 + 95 = 775
4. 475 + 76 = 551

Fill in the blanks to make the quantities represented on both sides of the equal sign the same.

5. 40 ÷ 10 = 20 ÷ 5
6. 8 × 8 = 16 × 4
7. 75 − 50 = 99 − 74
8. 15 ÷ 3 = 30 ÷ 6
9. 7 × 6 = 14 × 3
10. 120 − 95 = 145 − 120

Fill in the blank after each numbered problem with the letter of the correct solution. Try to solve these problems mentally.

11. 38 + 47 = B A. 248
12. 150 − 28 = C B. 85
13. 1000 − 752 = A C. 122
14. 855 − 245 = E D. 301
15. 150 + 151 = D E. 610

Arrange the numbers below each set of empty boxes inside the grid so that the number in the middle box is the result of multiplying the numbers to its right and left and also the result of multiplying the numbers above and below it. In each problem, there is one number that doesn't belong. Draw a ring around it.

	2	
3	12	4
	6	

16. 2, 3, 4, 6, (8), 12

	3	
5	30	6
	10	

17. 3, 5, 6, 10, 30, (35)

	2	
4	24	6
	12	

18. 2, 4, 6, 12, 24, (28)

© Houghton Mifflin Harcourt Publishing Company

MONTHLY ASSESSMENT

1. A rainbow displays colors in the order red, orange, yellow, green, blue, indigo, and violet. How many colors are displayed in 2 rainbows? 14
2. How many colors are displayed in 4 rainbows? 28
3. How many colors are displayed in 8 rainbows? 56

Write stories for each of these division sentences.

4. 25 ÷ 5 = 5 Answers will vary. Accept stories that show the division of 25 objects into 5 equal groups.
5. 15 ÷ 4 = 3 R3 Answers will vary. Accept stories that show sharing 15 objects in 4 equal groups with 3 left over.

For each of these problems, first tell whether you would use addition, subtraction, multiplication, or division to solve it. Then solve each problem.

6. Rita, Samantha, and Margarita each bought a bag of marbles at the store. Each bag had 10 marbles in it. How many marbles did they have all together? multiplication; 30
7. Kathy opened a carton of 12 eggs to make a cake. She discovered that 5 of the eggs were broken. How many unbroken eggs were left in the carton? subtraction; 7
8. Three friends were counting blue cars on different streets in their town. Tom saw 14. Miguel saw 9. Lee saw 8. How many cars did they count all together? addition; 31
9. Richard has ten pieces of gum to share with four of his friends. How many pieces of gum will each friend get? division; 2

MONTHLY ASSESSMENT

Who Am I?

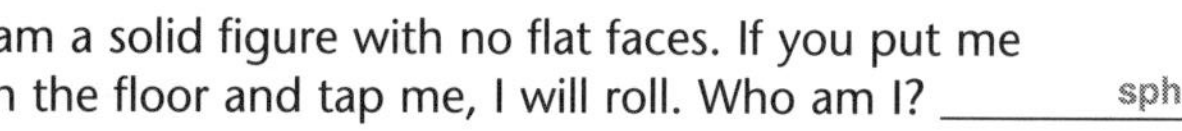

1. I am a solid figure with five faces. Four of my faces are the same and one is different. I have five corners. Who am I? pyramid
2. I am a solid figure with no flat faces. If you put me on the floor and tap me, I will roll. Who am I? sphere
3. I am a solid figure with only one flat face and a curved surface. Who am I? cone
4. I am a solid figure with eight square corners and six faces. My faces are not all the same size. Who am I? rectangular solid (box)

Draw a ring around the best answer.

5. What unit would you use to measure how much water is in a full fish tank?

   cup (quart)

6. What unit would you use to measure the width of your little finger?

   (centimeter) meter

7. What unit would you use to measure the distance from your knee to the floor?

   (foot) yard

8. What unit would you use to measure the weight of a small stone?

   (ounce) pound

9. What unit would you use to measure how much soda all the students in your school might drink in one week?

   milliliter (liter)

© Houghton Mifflin Harcourt Publishing Company

Teacher Notes